British Media
in a **Global Era**

British Media in a Global Era

Katharine Sarikakis

ARNOLD

First published in Great Britain in 2004 by
Arnold, a member of the Hodder Headline Group,
338 Euston Road, London NW1 3BH

http://www.arnoldpublishers.com

Distributed in the United States of America by
Oxford University Press Inc.
198 Madison Avenue, New York, NY10016

The advice and information in this book are believed to be true and accurate at the date of
going to press, but neither the author nor the publisher can accept any legal responsibility or
liability for any errors or omissions.

British Library Cataloguing in Publication Data
A catalogue record for this book is available from the British Library

Library of Congress Cataloguing-in-Publication Data
A catalog record for this book is available from the Library of Congress

ISBN 0 340 80733 4

1 2 3 4 5 6 7 8 9 10

Typeset in 10/12pt Garamond by Servis Filmsetting Ltd, Manchester
Printed and bound in Malta

What do you think about this book? Or any other Arnold title?
Please send your comments to feedback.arnold@hodder.co.uk

Contents

Foreword

The media in Britain: some thoughts from home

Martyn J. Lee

I suppose that the national media throughout all of the advanced industrial nations of the world today play a significant, if ultimately incalculable, role in shaping and articulating the sense of social and cultural identity of their citizenry. This relationship – between national media networks and national identities – is, even at an abstract and fairly generalized level, clearly a complex matter. It becomes positively labyrinthine, however, once we acknowledge that each national media network emerges from the unique social, cultural, economic, ethnic and political history, often dating back centuries, of the nation (or region) in question. Nowhere is this fact regarding the media's relationship with its audience more pertinent than in the case of Britain. What follows is a set of observations (no more than that), often (highly) personalized, regarding the role that the British media, but especially broadcast and printed media, play in defining not only notions of 'Britishness' but also the infinitely more complex issue of social and cultural identity generally.

These, then, are some 'thoughts from home' as it were, thoughts from someone who has been raised upon, immersed in, enlightened (and perhaps blinded) by British television, radio and newspapers in particular for over 40 years. It is hoped that this Foreword will provide a counter-measure to the rest of the book's text, which is written from the substantially advantageous standpoint of someone raised in another national media context and seeing the media in Britain with, shall we say, 'foreign', and therefore perhaps more perceptive, eyes.

At a very early age, one of the most powerful social facts I learned about British life was the manner in which issues of social class, and in particular class identification and allegiance, governed what seemed to be virtually every aspect of our everyday behaviour. Nowhere was this influence more keenly marked than in the national media that we consumed. Growing up in the late 1960s and early 1970s in the north of England I learned quickly that the daily newspaper read by my parents, the television programmes we tended to watch as a family and the radio stations we generally listened to represented far more than mere entertainments or factual sources of information, but stood as clear and visible statements about our class status (and perhaps more accurately about our class aspirations). I discovered at an early age, for example, that in matters of television choice one ought, at least if you regarded yourself as in some way middle class, to watch the BBC (or at least BBC1) rather than (the then still relatively new) ITV. The impression was that ITV was 'that channel watched by the (poorer) people across town', the folks who lived in council houses, who shopped in the cheaper stores and went to Blackpool on their holidays. Indeed, it became a long-standing joke among many aspiring middle-class families at that time that they had had the ITV button removed from their TV sets. We also took the *Daily Mail* because it seemed to 'speak for us', unlike newspapers such as the *Daily Mirror* or (worst of all) the *Sun* – I still remember vividly my father's outrage and genuine amazement when, at his workplace, he chanced upon a copy of the *Sun* left open at the topless model on page three. My suspicion was then, and is still now perhaps, that his distaste was focused not on the image of the bare breasts on the page but on the men who would want to buy and read such a newspaper.

Our family's attempts (and those of many like us) to distinguish and confirm their perceived class space through their media consumption also functioned in the opposite direction: if ITV was generally held to be a little too vulgar and downmarket for our tastes, then BBC2, with its emphasis on the Arts, and in particular the more radical and experimental Arts, quirky and surreal humour (for example, *Monty Python's Flying Circus*) and a more 'academic and learned' programming policy, was a little too highbrow, a little too intellectual – perhaps, dare I say, a little too boring. Without question this was, as later with the arrival of Channel 4 in 1982, a station that 'other people watched'.

Similarly when, from about the age of 16, I began to read the *Guardian* at home, I can still recall the way my father, in moments of idle curiosity, used to inspect the paper as though it were some museum document written in unintelligible Old English. (I confess, however, that I suspect that a prime reason why I began to read the *Guardian* in the first place was as an act of minor generational rebellion, a perceived need to move away from the class status of my parents.)

All of this makes my parents appear as class snobs, but the point is precisely this: my parents were by no means unusual in the precise nature of their media consumption. Nor was this sort of attention to the finer details of what one read, watched and listened to the preserve of my parents' class – all of the social groups I came into contact with and knew about when I was growing up had their own particular strategies of media discrimination. In short, the articulation of class status in Britain through media choices was – and, arguably, still is today – endemic, and at one level at least Britain is a nation of class snobs. It is simply part of the general 'social consciousness' of Britain and its 'class tribes'. If one is British, one hardly needs a degree qualification in Media Studies to identify the, often delicately and exquisitely drawn, lines of class demarcation between, say, the 'ideally imagined' readers of the *Sun*, the *Daily Mail*, the *Telegraph* and the *Guardian* newspapers. Nor are these ideally imagined readers the crude caricatures they are often portrayed as. On the face of it, for example, the differences in readership profiles of the *Sun* and the *Daily Mirror*, or the *Daily Mail* and the *Daily Express* are negligible (at least in material terms such as income and occupation type), yet the *cultural* distinctions between these various social constituencies are often sharp and, to the particular readerships in question (as well as the papers themselves), tangible and real: one does not switch from the *Sun* to the *Mirror*, or from the *Mail* to the *Express* without some extremely compelling reason. The most notable example of this was, perhaps, in the wake of the Hillsborough stadium football tragedy of 1989 when Liverpool supporters were somewhat maliciously accused by the *Sun* of directly contributing towards the deaths of 95 spectators. The *Sun* was boycotted by its regular readership throughout the city of Liverpool.

To understand what makes the character of indigenous British media so distinctive, then, I believe one needs to begin to appreciate the nature of the British class structure. In order to do this fully we need to begin to perceive class structure as being articulated along both a material and cultural axis. The model of class analysis adopted and developed by the French sociologist Pierre Bourdieu is perhaps closer to what I have in mind than more traditional notions of class (for perhaps the most systematic account of Bourdieu's analysis of social class, see in particular Bourdieu, P. (1984) *Distinction: A Social Critique of Taste*, RKP). In very broad terms Bourdieu rejects the usefulness of merely seeing notions of working-, middle- and upper-class constituencies as somewhat static and monolithic social 'blocs'. To see class in this way, particularly at the start of the twenty-first century, is to reduce the complex structure of class composition to a set of highly over-generalized and cartoon-like forms. Bourdieu operates with a far more finely variegated analytical model of class that sees class groupings as fractionally defined along intersecting dimensions of economic and cultural 'capital'. While economic capital is simply the stock of material wealth and possessions shared by members of particular social groups, it is the vital dimension of cultural capital, or the sum of cultural competences, skills and knowledge gained primarily through a relative access to the education system, that defines the precise character, disposition and sensibility of each class group or class fraction. Moreover, these class fractions (Bourdieu writes of the French class system, for example, as containing groups such as the petite bourgeoisie, the new petite bourgeoisie, etc.) are in a perpetual struggle with those closest to them in cultural terms to establish a certain superiority or sense of 'distinction'. In short, class groupings are at any particular moment situated along a trajectory of either upward or downward mobility in contrast to those groups with whom they are in direct competition.

In the case of Britain, at least operating with a broadly similar model of class structure begins to make intelligible the vagaries of its indigenous media forms. A fictional example, I think, demonstrates this well. In an episode of Steve Coogan's series *I'm Alan Partridge*, the insufferable C-list media 'celebrity' and local radio DJ Alan Partridge (a fictional creation so obsessed with defining the precise boundaries of his particular petit bourgeois class location that it becomes virtually an art form for him) encounters his soulmate for the first time at a petrol station. After a quick exchange where the two (equally obnoxious) characters compare their preferences and possessions, Alan is finally confirmed in his admiration for his new-found friend when he spies a copy of the *Daily Mail* under his friend's arm. This is no accident, for the *Daily Mail*, arguably like any newspaper, becomes an extreme but quite precise shorthand for the cultural-class sensibility of its readership.

While, to my mind, class is perhaps the overarching social fact that determines the character of British media, it is of course by no means the exclusive determinant of this

Increasingly over recent years other demographic factors have assumed a growing significance. In the field of radio broadcasting, for example, age, arguably more than any other factor, has shaped programming and policy decisions profoundly. If one looks, for instance, at the manner in which the BBC's Radio 2 successfully relaunched itself during the mid- to late 1990s in terms of a radically new target listener constituency, then it is clear that factors connected primarily with age were paramount in the station's redesign. Radio 2 had always, at least throughout the 1970s and 1980s, been seen as unashamedly middle of the road; the station became a byword for listeners who were middle aged, middle class, conservative, conventional and perhaps somewhat 'boring'. Today Radio 2 has attempted to throw off this image, while at the same time continuing to base its conception of its 'ideal listener' as, first and foremost, someone defined by their age (typically someone in either their forties or early fifties). Radio 2 barely disguises the fact that its listeners are seen as those people who listened to Radio 1 during the late 1960s and throughout the 1970s and have now graduated, by virtue of nothing other than the fact that they have 'grown up', to Radio 2. Whereas the audience distinction between Radios 1 and 2 used to be based loosely on a notion of generational conflict, today that notion of conflict is represented as merely a 'maturing of listening tastes': at the risk of over-simplification one might suggest that Radio 2 sees itself as simply 'Radio 1 for grown-ups'. A glance at the station's current DJs tends to confirm this view. While several of the 'old guard' of presenters remain and undoubtedly cater for the much older listener (for example, David Jacobs, Richard Baker, Humphrey Lyttelton, Ken Bruce and Terry Wogan), Radio 2's promotional push has very much been to emphasize its new vibrant breed of DJ, many of whom previously worked for Radio 1 in the 1970s and 1980s (for example, Janice Long, Johnnie Walker, Noel Edmonds, Paul Gambaccini, Simon Mayo and Steve Wright), or were pop stars themselves in the 1970s and 1980s (Suzi Quatro, Mica Paris, Jools Holland and Steve Harley) or have had parallel TV careers in somewhat 'alternative' programmes (Mark Lamarr, Jonathan Ross and Stuart Maconie).

The issue of radio audiences in Britain, or more accurately their conception by radio's policy-makers, is indeed interesting for its emphasis on age as a primary determinant. It has long since struck me that unlike TV, where individual stations seek to appeal to a broader audience constituency with a much more diverse programming policy, radio stations in general tend to determine their policy around the idea of 'regular listeners', who are identified perhaps first and foremost by their age. This fact is probably determined by the very different cultural uses of TV and radio.

What emerges from all of this is a glimpse of how the BBC fundamentally positions itself in relation to a perceived popular audience, not just in radio broadcasting but arguably in its broadcasting policy generally. Class and age seem to me to be the two primary factors that govern the BBC's national output (whatever their relative merits, Radios 3 and 4, for example, are unashamedly and unmistakably middle class and middle aged in their mode of audience address and their programming policies). What is spectacularly lacking here is virtually any serious attempt even to acknowledge racial and ethnic audience diversity among its viewers and listeners. When, on the extremely rare occasion, the BBC creates programmes for a non-white audience, its efforts are generally perceived as rather ham-fisted, patronizing and amateurish.

To be sure much of this problem stems from the enormous cultural weight bestowed on the BBC by its illustrious history. Even if we leave aside the massive impact of the BBC's cultural legacy abroad, it is still clear that for its domestic audiences the BBC's general cultural 'mind-set' (what Bourdieu might refer to as its 'habitus') is profoundly conditioned by the enormous historical circumstance of its pioneering role as the first national public service broadcaster. This 'cultural weight' is far more than imaginary. As the crucible of the BBC's primary identity, its monumental role in shaping public opinion during the Second World War (see Chapter 1) established a set of powerful cultural responsibilities that, even today, it finds difficult to move away from: its primary remit to 'inform' and 'educate' ('to entertain' has always been of secondary stature), its 'trustworthiness', its 'authority', in short, its paternalism. Not that these factors have been by any means wholly problematic for the BBC; it enjoys an almost unrivalled audience respect among public service broadcasting everywhere in the world where typically such broadcasting is regarded by its audiences as either somewhat 'worthy and dull' compared to the far more glamorous commercial networks (as is the case of RAI in Italy), or as perhaps tarnished by its association with past/present unpopular state or government political regimes (as is the case, for example, with Greek public service broadcasting).

In matters of news, debate and information, the BBC by contrast, at home at least, enjoys a supreme reputation. A perhaps tacit but common perception is sometimes thought to exist that an event has not actually happened *until* it has been reported on by the BBC. In matters of national and international crisis, or significant home or world events the BBC is still regularly the source that, at least statistically, a majority of the British people turn to for their news. Moreover this tag of trustworthiness and authority has, in spite of numerous protestations from many diverse quarters, historically, been reinforced because the BBC is popularly perceived as genuinely independent from both political affiliation (in particular from the government of the day) and from commercial control. It is, to quote a recent example, far from accidental that the journalists at the heart of the Hutton Inquiry into the death of the government scientist David Kelly were both BBC journalists from the two BBC flagship news programmes (Andrew Gilligan from Radio 4's *Today* and Susan Watts of BBC2's *Newsnight*). Indeed, the whole impetus of the Hutton Inquiry soon became driven, not by issues about the war in Iraq, but by a monumental battle between the Labour government and the BBC itself, and fought over the ground of the integrity of each institution. Without wishing to downplay the seriousness of the issues at stake, one strongly suspects that if the original unauthorized briefing had been to journalists not from the BBC then the whole affair would have unfolded very differently. In short, for many ordinary people Lord Hutton's Inquiry became a fundamental litmus test of which of the two primary national institutions (the government or the BBC) one trusted the most, and it is debatable that any other broadcasting network in the world could have provoked such a significant situation.

Here we arrive at what is perhaps the crux of the whole issue of the media in Britain: the overwhelming imprint left by the BBC, not just upon other media in Britain, but crucially upon the 'consciousnesses' of the British public. The old adage that 'the BBC is simply Britain talking to itself' still retains a very strong resonance. In fact it is perhaps inconceivable to imagine a Britain without the BBC, and by this I don't just mean a media system without the BBC but indeed a national culture without the BBC. For better or for worse, to be born and raised in Britain inevitably means having to negotiate a complex nexus of national cultural attitudes and sensibilities that have been and continue to be in no small measure articulated, mediated and shaped by the BBC. This is in no way meant necessarily to imply that the BBC is universally culturally adored by the British people (national cultural attitudes are always far more complex and contradictory in character than this notion could ever allow for); indeed, its underlying conservatism, its unashamed paternalism, its historical ties to 'the establishment' and to notions of empire, its inability to address seriously anything other than a perceived British cultural 'middle ground' (i.e. one that is essentially white, middle class and middle aged) is often held up for ridicule and disdain. Nonetheless the BBC, rather like a parent one often disapproves of or is embarrassed by, remains bound up in essence as an integral aspect of 'Britishness'. In this respect it shapes profoundly the national cultural landscape on which all other British and British-based media organizations, whatever their remit or political or commercial orientation and affiliation, must situate themselves.

Coventry
December 2003

Acknowledgements

I believe there is hardly anything on this planet that can be regarded as the work of a sole individual, as most works are the result of the valuable contributions and good will of many people. For this book, many people have offered help – from those who have provided the sources for necessary material to those who made sure the sentences make sense. But since my name will be on the cover of this book, the least I can do is to acknowledge the collective work of colleagues, some of whom I did not have the pleasure to meet face to face; their help has been invaluable throughout this project: the editors at Arnold for suggesting and supporting the writing of this text, and all those who helped turn the manuscript into the book you are now holding in your hands; Dr Chris Atton, Andrew Beck, Dr Bob Bennett, Dr Michael Higgins and Dr Myra MacDonald, who have graciously and generously offered me helpful comments and insightful views; Sumati Nagrath, who is always there with suggestions and sharp comments; Ken Faro, the director of *Injustice* for interview and material; my students, who have asked the right questions; Martyn Lee, whose contribution provides the canvas of this work; and, of course, the most precious people in my life, for they are always there and make work worth doing and life worth living. I thank them all. Responsibility for the content is mine.

Katharine Sarikakis
February 2004

Introduction

When I was first approached to write a book about the British media from an international perspective, it was clear to me what the book should look like: it would be an exploration of the international dimensions of the British media. But when I looked more closely at my mandate, a number of questions surfaced about the breadth and depth of this exploration. What kind of media shall I be exploring? What makes them British? What does *from an 'international' perspective* mean?

I took a step back and tried to trace the 'moments' and the media I have experienced as someone who was not raised in this country. I have vague memories of the BBC, my first experience of the British media in my home country (Greece). I remember my parents tuning in to the BBC's Greek service, along with Deutsche Welle towards the end of the military dictatorship (1967–73), to catch a glimpse of 'what was happening in the world' and perhaps to hear some news about our own country. I was only three years old, so it was only later that I understood the context of our evening listening. I did not know or understand anything about the BBC or the dictatorship, but I remember sensing some uncomfortable emotions, as if listening to the radio was something we were not supposed to be doing. Later, when I could put these experiences into context, I realized that these were the feelings people have when they are forced to hide the fact that they are accessing information they are not supposed to have (my parents were careful not to turn up the volume). When I was growing up I remember the radio or television news sometimes quoting Reuters and the BBC, and during my adolescence it became clear to me that these were trustworthy sources. Later, when I became a journalist myself, I tuned in to the BBC (not the Greek service this time) to catch news that was not necessarily reported in the Greek press.

How, then, do the eyes of a non-native British person (a scholar and a consumer) see the British media? The answer is clear: the BBC is the British media. *The Times* ('of London' as it is sometimes, inaccurately, referred to) is the British press. However, once ensconced here, one has to try to come to terms with the unbearably unglamorous *Coronation Street*, the mercilessly uninteresting BBC2 on a Saturday night, the (only occasionally these days) provocative Channel 4, the dustbin known as the *Sun*, and the oppositional and interesting – although often dry and old-fashioned – *New Internationalist*. Of course, these are only impressions and not intended to offer a scholarly critique of the quality of the British media. They tend to reflect, however, a certain socioeconomic background or class, and probably gender. Such superficial statements may also give a clue as to the forms of media with which one is most familiar.

Certainly, one cannot claim scholarly engagement with the subject unless one delves deeper into the structures and ideas that have shaped the media. Easy labels aside, this book will try to map the ways in which we can begin to see the British media from an international perspective. It will look at how a variety of sources discuss the British media, as well as at original research, and will aim to highlight those elements that demonstrate two things: first, the 'internationality' of the British media themselves, mainly thanks to that grand institution that is the BBC; second, the role of the world, international economic structures and multinational corporations, among others, in shaping the media landscape in Britain. For this reason, the book asks questions such as 'Who owns the "British" media?', 'How successful are the British media in the international market and with international audiences?', 'What does it mean to carry "British" content?' and 'Who makes up the "British" public and where can we find it in this process of shaping the media landscape?'

We will start our exploration of British media in a global era with an overview of the historical development of the media, as discussed in Chapter 1. The chapter seeks to provide a general picture of the ways in which media and communications are largely defined as 'British' – because their ownership is in principle British and/or because they are controlled by the British state. Furthermore, it aims to identify a few under-emphasized, until now, perspectives of the history of the British media and relate this historical trajectory to the worlds of politics, economy and the military. In doing so, this exploration addresses the position of the British Empire, and therefore its media, in the world, social dynamics as expressed through class and gender relations, and the role of wars in providing the background against which the British media established themselves as world players. This chapter (along with the Foreword) should be seen as providing a context from within which the reader of contemporary British media can embark on the study of more specific aspects in the following chapters. The reader is also encouraged to look carefully at Table 1.1 and reflect on the history of the development of the British media as affected by state policy in the period 1923–90. This table offers some examples of major social, cultural, economic and political events in Britain and the world, and reveals the multiple levels of interaction and influence between the general Zeitgeist of each period and the possible effect of these on the direction of changes in the media.

Chapter 2 goes on to examine the contemporary media system in Britain, from the 1990s onwards. It locates British media and cultural products in the world, and addresses the factors that help them maintain a position of dominance in the global market. The relationship between British and international media is examined in terms of content, ownership and technology. Some British-made media products, such as *Who Wants to Be a Millionaire?*, have enjoyed enormous success with international audiences; on the other hand, programmes such as *A Touch of Frost* are mostly only successful in (and directed at) the 'local' market. The chapter discusses the importance of cultural proximity for the consumption of cultural goods. Similarly, US-originated content, and in particular film, appear to have become the most important 'foreign' presence on British audiovisual media. The chapter seeks to introduce questions that explore 'how British' the British media really are, given that the industry is generally foreign-owned or has strong transnational links. These trends – 'foreign' ownership, the dominance of Hollywood, use of the Internet as, predominantly, just another 'shopping centre' – are observed on an international scale. The chapter also examines how the development of the media industries elsewhere has affected the media 'at home'.

What has the response of the state been to the globalization of the economy, the internationalization of media content and the expansion of the Internet? Can Britain still claim a 'national' system of media decision-making or are other systems currently important in the process of policy-making? Chapters 3 and 4 approach Britain in its multipolarity as a world player that has to work with other countries while, of course, adhering to certain forms of international law. Britain belongs (albeit somehow reluctantly) to the greater 'European' family; it participates in the decision-making of the EU and is, similarly, expected to respect policies agreed at EU level. Despite politicians' (and national newspapers') attempts to foster anti-European and even xenophobic sentiments, European citizens do share British cultural heritage(s) and are contributing to a new form of 'Britishness' – indeed 'Europeanness' – as are the many Britons who live and work in continental Europe. Similarly, EU law is accepted by the British state and often shapes the framework within which national policies are formed. These chapters examine media policy in Britain, the historical context of major international policy issues and the ways in which the British regulator has attempted to address them. The most important policies – such as the Broadcasting Acts of 1990 and 1996, and the 2002 Communications Bill – are discussed in Chapter 4.

Chapter 5 turns its attention to an often disregarded sector of the media landscape: the public. In this chapter, the public is approached in its role as audience, consumer and citizen. The relationship between the media and the public is examined, as is the role of the public in media policy-making and its relationship with the regulators. Some of the issues discussed here are the right to have one's dignity protected and the right to reply. The overarching question addressed is whether the public has any major role to play in the shaping of the British media.

Expanding on this discussion of the relationship between the public and the media, Chapter 6 seeks to address grassroots roles in the production and consumption of alternative forms of media in Britain. Often, studies of the British media fail to acknowledge that environmental groups, the feminist movement, civil rights groups and others have a rich tradition in Britain in making and distributing their own media. If one accepts that something 'hasn't happened unless it is reported on by the BBC' or the other mainstream media, then one understands the significance of alternative media in providing a plurality of views that would otherwise have remained obscured by the dominance of the big media companies. The 'Others' of the British media are radical and alternative presses that are seldom commercially successful but that significantly amend history as written by the mainstream and elite media.

Finally, in Chapter 7, the reader will find three separate case studies that encompass the main themes explored in the book. These are:

- a discussion of the film *Injustice*, a documentary that follows the lives of family members of people who have died in police custody in Britain

- an exploration of the links between the porn industry and mainstream media in the UK
- a discussion about the role and image of the BBC in the international community.

These case studies draw on issues of policy, ownership, content and 'identity', and will help readers identify connections between the superficially different factors that shape today's British media landscape.

chapter one

A look at the past

The British media in the world

The current landscape and character of the media in Britain have developed through events that are historically linked in their technological, political, social and cultural dimensions. So that we may better understand the present organization of the British media, it is important for us to know something of their history. A look at the past will provide the background against which we can study British media in their current form and also make predictions about their likely future.

There are several 'histories' of the British media that can be examined: the history of the growth of different genres in radio, the history of television, the chronological changes in the development of media ownership, or the history of media 'heroes' and pioneers. These are just some potential areas of interest. This book will mainly concentrate on the relationship of the British media with the world. This means that our main focus will be on the interaction between British media and international political, social and economic developments. It is not only the current position occupied by the British media in the international market, but also their national role that is firmly rooted in the history of Great Britain as a colonial/military power and participant in international politics. Studying the media in this context will help to highlight important aspects of their role, such as their cultural significance, their relationship to other nations and the effects of other histories on that of the British media.

British media and the Empire

Communication has long been used extensively by political and economic powers to assert their position in the world. States have depended upon the media to investigate and provide information about military forces, resources and costs, to transmit orders and control remote territories. They have also used their own national media as agents that have helped project particular versions of national identity and even 'create' particular versions of national and world history. Empires, from the ancient world to the present day, have used communication networks to maintain or increase power internally or in relation to 'foreign' powers. During wars – but also in trading enterprises – the technologies of the day have been used to facilitate communication systems in a race against time and space. The media current in each historical period, whether bard or town crier, messenger, letter, the telegraph or the Internet, have provided a support system that has enabled the coordination of activities, the exchange of information and ideas, and the creation and promotion of cultural and national identities.

The media were a crucial factor in the unification of the British Empire in the nineteenth century (Thussu 2000: 14). A system of communication networks, created and revolutionized thanks to the invention and use of the telegraph, put the British Empire in an advanced position compared to its world competitors. The history of the media illustrates their political and economic uses from the era of the British Empire to the present. By 1851 the first public telegraph service in Britain was catering for the transfer of money orders and information about the price of raw materials and resources, and conveyed commands and political decisions from the centre to the colonies at a much faster pace than had previously been possible. British merchants benefited from the new technologies available and were able to compete for better prices on the market. Wars and military operations depended on and were assisted by new communications – the new media of the time – such as the first trans-Pacific cable, which was used during the war between Japan and Russia of 1904–05. This cable, co-owned by Australia, Britain, Canada and New Zealand, connected Vancouver to Sydney and Brisbane (Thussu 2000: 17). The dominance of international communications meant a privileged position in the world economy of the time and provided military advantage.

By the end of the First World War, Britain was already a world media power, having dominated the telegraph systems (Marconi) and cable companies through ownership. Read (1992) and Thussu (2000) point out the power of Great Britain in indirectly censoring the communications travelling through its cables by diplomatic means. Britain had control over the markets of raw materials for the production of cables. The British colonial government promoted the development of cable technology through scientific knowledge or financial support, as did other colonial governments, but the ownership of the means of production of cables and transmission belonged to private companies. Together with the USA, Great Britain owned and controlled 75 per cent of the world's cables (Thussu 2000). This meant that the country had control of communications at different levels: it had ownership control, which further allowed the control of content transmission, as well as control over the direction and prioritization of technological development. Becoming – and remaining – a world superpower depended a great deal on the ability to control not only the means of communication, but also the technology and content of communication systems.

The lords of the press

Meanwhile, the rise of the news agencies in the late 1880s signalled a new era in the systematization of news-gathering and dissemination of news at an international level. The system of news agencies had an enormous impact on communication, both international and national. The establishment of the news agencies Reuters (UK) and Associated Press (USA), mainly facilitated by cable technology, changed both the international and the British media landscapes. Newspapers relied on the news agencies to provide them with correspondence from the colonies. Reuters, the most powerful news agency, and world news leader until 1914, also became the major source of financial and industrial information.

The rise of Reuters coincided with the rise of the industrial press and the beginnings of the concentration of press ownership. Towards the end of the nineteenth century, new printing technologies further reduced the cost of newspaper production. The linotype machine replaced web rotary machines in the 1880s and 1890s, press taxes were lifted and a slight improvement in the living standards of the working classes boosted the press in Britain. However, at the same time, the costs involved in actually establishing a newspaper rose dramatically, making it impossible for those with limited capital to enter the market.

Although multiple ownership of the press goes back to the seventeenth century, the late nineteenth century was the era of the 'press barons'. This was the age when conglomerates were built around newspaper businesses, with the establishment of multiple publications and other related enterprises. However, it was with the industrialization of press production, which replaced the craft mode, that the high costs of establishing and launching a new publication made it impossible for new voices to enter the market (Curran and Seaton 1997, 2003). The industrialization of the press heralded the characteristics that can still be seen in the modern press today: advertising revenue, a focus on entertainment at the expense of information provision, multiple and cross-ownership, a large number of publications and media in the hands of a smaller number of owners, and the marginalization of other presses (such as the radical press).

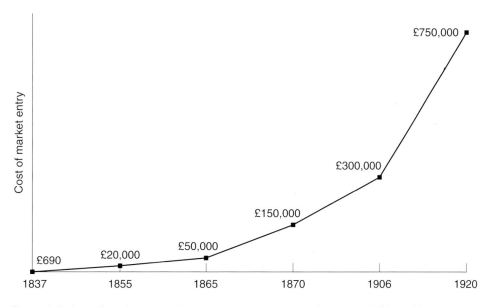

Figure 1.1 Cost of market entry during the industrialization of the press, 1837–1920
Source: adapted from Curran and Seaton 1997

Figure 1.1 shows the increasing cost of launching a new newspaper in London. Between 1850 and 1920, in order for newspapers to break even they had to increase their circulation by over 4000 per cent! While the *Northern Star* was able to break even with 6200 copies sold in 1837, the *Sunday Express* sold over 250,000 copies to cover its costs (Curran and Seaton

1997). The consequence of these increased costs was that the press now depended on distribution systems and circulation tactics, such as the use of graphics, which in turn led to additional costs.

The railway, the telegraph and the modern corporation ushered in the first media moguls on both sides of the Atlantic. In the USA, similar market and technological conditions to those in Great Britain boosted the production of new titles and, between 1880 and 1889, the largest ten-year increase in the history of the US press. Rogers (1998: 51) describes the American experience as follows:

> It was a bloody period of mergers and acquisitions as wrenching and fast paced as anything we're witnessing today. Hearst was notorious for moving into cities, purchasing existing papers and then shutting them down or folding them into his empire. . . . The owner of a newspaper had to supply it with newsprint, ink, staff and stories. The same owner with 20 papers could centralize his accounting functions, his sources of supply and his news gathering.

The (limited) freedom of the press, and the radical papers

Concentration of ownership, the increase in advertising revenue and technological development that allowed the use of sources other than political parties and the government gave the press a certain independence from the state. Newspapers like *The Times* proudly pronounced their independence from governmental sources as early as 1834 (Curran and Seaton 1997, 2003) and asserted themselves as products of independent rational thinking, of the ideals of the Enlightenment. Advocacy of the values of the Enlightenment – equality and the power of reason – were to become the foremost traits of a 'free press'. This did not mean, however, that a free press was born. Often considered to be the 'fourth estate', which exercises critique and questions those in power, the press (and in particular the mainstream press) does not necessarily cover the news in a way that serves equality among citizens or offers argument that is free of prejudice. The roots of the fourth estate can be traced to the ideals of the Enlightenment in terms of the 'Declaration of the Rights of Man', which gave rise to the establishment of a number of radical publications in the eighteenth century and which were reinforced further thanks to the opportunities presented by the technological developments of the nineteenth century.

It is important to note that when Rogers (1998) refers to the press owner, she means the *male* press owner. Although humanistic ideals of equality and natural rights prevailed in the British, other European and American press, these were not seen to extend to women. Those who advocated women's rights were marginalized and often silenced using violence. Addressing the shortcomings of the male-dominated Enlightenment project, Olympe de Gouge, a French revolutionary, was executed by guillotine in 1793 on a charge of treason. De Gouge wrote the 'Declaration of the Rights of Woman and Female Citizen' to challenge the assumed inferiority of women in the 'Rights of Man' and called for freedom for women, including equality and choice in matters of marriage and procreation (de Gouge 1979). By 1880, almost a century later, the sentiments towards women's freedom had not changed dramatically, at least as seen by the state and the mainstream press. Annie Besant, one of the early women journalists and writers, was attacked on grounds of morality. She was an English journalist, whose work *The Laws of Population*, which advocated birth control, was characterized by *The Times* as 'indecent, filthy and obscene' (www.spartacus. schoolnet.co.uk).

In the late nineteenth century, then, the press was a male-dominated domain. However, the impact of the suffragette movement for women's right to vote, equal access to education and work grew steadily, and with it more women entered the fields of journalism and public communication. It was in the realm of the radical press, which played a catalytic role in eighteenth- and the first half of nineteenth-century Britain, that women found fertile ground from which to write, advocate, socialize and lead political and ideological struggles. Between 1852 and 1868 Harriet Martineau, an influential English social reformer, wrote 1600 articles for the *Daily News* both as a foreign correspondent on American affairs and as a political commentator (Martineau Society). Radical thinkers and reformers also used the radical press to advocate social change and they often founded new publications. One such publication was the radical newspaper, *The Link*, founded by Annie Besant in London; it played a leading role in the Matchgirls' Union and the workers' strike at the Bryant & May factory in 1888 (www.spartacus.schoolnet.co.uk). Later, Besant moved to India and founded a weekly newspaper, the *Commonwealth*, and renamed another, *New India*, in 1914. Both publications advocated self-rule for India, 'Home Rule' as it became known, and the right of people in the colonies to vote.

At the beginning of the twentieth century, further technological developments made possible the introduction of the next 'new medium' of the era: the kinematograph. This new medium caused further worries for the state. Film and the cinema attracted mainly young people, the unemployed and the working classes, and more women than men. By 1914 annual cinema admissions were at 364 million (Corrigan in Eldridge *et al.* 1997: 14). Clearly this was a mass and popular medium. Film was particularly appealing to women, as cinemas had become one of the very few, if not only, public places in which women could socialize. Rather like the moral panics spread today about the detrimental effects of the Internet on the moral values of our society, were ideas about the 'corrupting' effect of the new media of the time: the cinema. These moral panics were constructed as a reaction to the unexpected success of cinema among 'vulnerable' social strata. Women, seen as the weaker sex – weak in upholding high morals and in constant need of control, especially in terms of sexuality – were populating cinemas and watching romantic films. While, today, this is an acceptable and widespread social activity, at the time it disturbed dominant ideas about the spaces women were allowed to 'occupy' and who had control over their leisure time. The state – in the form of the 'forces of morality' such as churches and teachers, and the elite classes – was alarmed by this mass medium it saw as a threat to the social order, and soon made sure to gain control over the kind of films that were shown.

Later, by the 1930s, cinema-goers were predominantly women and young people, which was reflected in the exhibitors' choice of films, mainly love and romantic stories, and horror films. Again, the increasing participation of women was used to fuel rhetorical claims about the deterioration of moral order, a discourse led by the governing elites. The cinema entrepreneurs, however, were profiting from the success of this new medium and did not want to jeopardize their businesses. In 1912 they formed the voluntary British Board of Film Censors (BBFC), which issued rules on a number of topics that could not be shown, among which were relationships between white girls and men of 'other races', women in a state of intoxication and Bolshevik propaganda. The reason behind this voluntary censorship was that the cinema industrialists wanted to avoid state intervention in their businesses. The only way to achieve this would be by proving that they could be 'trusted' or, in other words, through self-regulation (Eldridge *et al.* 1997).

Meanwhile, the radical papers, such as those mentioned above but also including others such as the *Political Register* and the *Poor Man's Guardian*, helped develop a nationwide consciousness among the working class by promoting working-class organizations, and giving visibility to their working and living conditions. Moreover, the consumption of the radical press became a form of communication ritual, with people forming queues to buy the papers and then discuss their content, which in turn led to a mobilization of the masses that demanded social change. The radical press also helped the working-class movement to develop sophisticated political analysis, and to redefine social and economic relations (Curran and Seaton 1997, 2003). However, with the industrialization of the press and the dominance of the wealthy press houses, the radical and local press faced extinction. Local papers were bought by industrialists, and the press shifted towards liberal, middle-class consensual journalism as opposed to its early militant and critical stance. Through the strategy of minimizing difference between the ruling and the working classes, blocking out conflict and encouraging positive identification with middle-class leadership, the liberal press contributed to the disorganization of the working-class movement (Curran and Seaton 1997; 2003). Examples of this change can be found in the way that newspapers reported on the British Empire: Britain's colonial rule was portrayed as 'enlightener of underdeveloped nations and civilizer of savage worlds'. Reuters, the 'unofficial voice of the Empire', projected the British view on international affairs but also in national politics in its colonies (Thussu 2000).

The increase in trade and expansion of European capitalism brought with it the need for more commercial news, which was served by Reuters. By the end of the First World War, the media dominating the British market were controlled by a few representatives of the interests of the ruling classes, such as lords and industrialists. Due to the 'structured' nature of this environment, the movements for women's and class emancipation did not find friendly representations within the mainstream press, which was eager to maintain its readership through the homogenization of its audiences by promoting undifferentiated politics. This line was inclined to support rather than challenge the status quo. The media further collaborated with the establishment in the construction of a national identity, based on fantasies of consensus and homogeneity among social strata and the superiority of the British as a civilizing force. In 1911 the British government and Reuters made a secret arrangement to circulate official speeches across the Empire for an annual fee of £500, courtesy of the Colonial Office. Another arrangement, to similar effect, was made with the Foreign Office and was to see the establishment of a wartime news service (Thussu 2000: 22).

The colonization of the 'new' and old media in the interwar period: state and capital

In 1926 the British Broadcasting Corporation (BBC) was born, as a non-profit, public-interest broadcasting monopoly, while at the same time the USA was developing its own radio culture based on the commercial model. The aim of the BBC – to serve the public interest – was to provide an influential public radio model across Europe. The governments of economically powerful countries saw radio as the ideal medium through which to dispense their propaganda. Through radio, they would transfer messages beyond boundaries and without the need for bilateral agreements between countries. They made sure to occupy and take control of the limited radio spectrum (mainly Britain, the USA, Germany, France and Russia) without considering other countries. The Russian communist, German Nazi and Italian fascist governments used radio for the dissemination of ideological propaganda through transmissions in other languages (German radio, for instance, was broadcast in 50 other languages). Although British radio cultivated an image of independence from the government, this was more myth than reality. Curran and Seaton (1997: 123) described the 1930s' BBC as follows.

> In a decade of hunger marches and 'red united fighting fronts' the BBC regarded a succession of royal broadcasts as the triumph of outside broadcasting and actuality reporting. Broadcasting in the 1930s was dominated by state openings, royal anniversaries, visits, deaths and births, and by the Coronation.

Not only did the BBC become defensive, insensitive to trades unions and fail to manage to reflect the problems facing British society, it also remained dependent on the government's content-related decisions. The BBC's Empire Service (later to become the World Service) was broadcast in 7 languages in 1932 and 39 by the end of the Second World War. Through this service, the broadcaster also cultivated a 'modern' image of the monarchy that reached all corners of the Empire. Finally, the production side of the BBC was not as humane and egalitarian as the Corporation would have liked it to appear (Curran and Seaton 1997). Although it was women who had set up key departments at the launching of BBC (the Education Service and Talks Department by Mary Somerville and Hilda Matheson respectively), most women working for the corporation were assigned secretarial duties. Barely a quarter of the total female staff was active in creative or senior administrative positions. Hilda Matheson was the founder of radio journalism and the first woman to write a book on broadcasting. She was responsible for the promotion and development of cultural and high-quality journalism. The deeply embedded sexism of the Corporation, however, made it impossible for her to continue her work and she eventually resigned over the censorship of 'Talks'.

It was not only the BBC, however, that refused to respond to social problems. By the 1930s, the BBFC had banned films that depicted conflict between labour and capital, strikes, or indeed any other issues that would question the social order and production relationships. Similarly, the mainstream press controlled by the moguls of the times was hostile to movements that challenged the social order, such as trade unionism and radical opponents of the government, and redirected attention away from the problems in British society such movements were addressing. Furthermore, the economic demands placed on newspaper production created new kinds of dependencies for the press and closed the door to potential new voices: for 20 years (between 1919 and 1939) not a single newspaper managed to enter the market. The communist *Sunday Worker* was boycotted by distributors and forced to settle for a marginal circulation.

Meanwhile, the buying power of the working class had increased. The emergence of sophisticated methods of audience research and analysis on behalf of the advertisers revealed new economic possibilities. The press realized that in order to attract more advertising, it had to appeal to the concerns of the working classes. This was achieved mainly in a non-threatening way, by providing greater support for reformist politics, while at the same time reducing the volume of political and industrial pages, and devoting more column inches to entertainment, 'women's interests' and youth. The *Daily Mirror* was the first to relaunch itself, becoming a (commercially) successful model for other papers to follow (Curran and Seaton 1997).

The Second World War: moments of freedom for women and the press

During the early years of the Second World War, a part of the press led anti-war campaigns by shedding light on the inadequacies of the country in preparing for war and also by criticizing military involvement, which was seen to have imperialist and capitalist motivations. The left-wing press had become increasingly critical of the government but had also supported a victorious war. Churchill's government issued a censorship law, Regulation 2D, which forbade the press to express opinions that would endanger victory in the war in which the government was engaged. In an attempt to silence criticism, the government closed down two communist papers (the *Daily Worker* and the *Week*) and exercised pressure on the left-wing *Daily Mirror* and *Sunday Pictorial* to change course to a more favourable government line (Curran and Seaton 1997). This created controversy in Parliament, but also drew a reaction from the majority of editors of daily newspapers, who supported the two newspapers. The power of the newspapers, with a combined circulation of 2 million, and the resistance of the press to what they saw as an attack on the liberty of the press and their own interests made the government withdraw its pressure and lift the ban on the *Daily Worker*. As Curran and Seaton point out (1997: 67), it was the *ideal* of the liberal press that opposed Churchill's authoritarian policy and the work of activists that maintained the tradition of a free press.

Despite such restrictive policies, during the Second World War women and the radical press found a space to break away from the press market and the social margins imposed on them. After the First World War (in 1918), having fought for the right to vote for almost two centuries, women who were property owners over 30 years of age were allowed to vote. Their contribution to the First World War effort made the value of women's work too visible to be ignored and it was no longer feasible for them to be denied political rights. In 1928 British women won the right to vote at 21 years of age, the same age as men, with Margaret Bondfield becoming the first woman cabinet minister a year later. During the interwar period, society's perceptions about women entering education and having the same rights as men relaxed. Many educated women pursued careers as writers and journalists. When the Second World War broke out, women wanted to report from the front line. More often than not, it was not a simple task to persuade their editors to assign them the job and, after that, to overcome prejudices and obstacles on the part of their male colleagues and the military. Some of them had to emigrate to gain the right to be sent to the front. Iris Carpenter, a journalist for the *Daily Express* and the *Daily Herald*, moved to the United States to become a war correspondent for the *Boston Globe*, as did Tania Long, who among other events covered the Blitz in London and the D-Day landings (Wagner 1989). Barbara M. Finch, who worked for Reuters, was also one of the accredited women war correspondents (Library of Congress).

Because of a paper shortage, the mainstream press had to reduce the amount of advertising they accepted. The pages were reduced to one-third of their former size, which also meant a reduction in the amount of entertainment material included, and an increase in items on war and public affairs. Newspapers like the *Daily Mirror*, not having to appeal to larger audiences, concentrated on their most homogenized audience: the working class. The radical press, also free from advertising and circulation pressures and economically relieved, was able to grow; the *Daily Mirror, Sunday Pictorial, Daily Herald, Reynolds News* and *Daily Worker* had a combined circulation of 9 million in 1945 (Curran and Seaton 1997: 69). It was due to the state's economic intervention to ensure equitable distribution of the press that radical journalism was revived in the war years.

The Second World War was also the time when the explosion of radio propaganda and the increase of news agencies' significance for the same reasons marked media history. By 1939, 25 countries were broadcasting to other countries in several languages. Radio technology was inexpensive, however, and this made the medium popular and its use widespread. During the war, the BBC helped the American military to establish the America Forces Network and broadcast programmes for US troops in Britain, the Middle East and Africa (Thussu 2000: 28). In 1942 Voice of America (VOA) radio took over the role of addressing American audiences and promoting US government policies.

The Cold War era

After the end of the Second World War, another war commenced: the Cold War. This war was fought not only on the battlefield, with invasions of a number of 'third world' countries and accelerated militarization, it also stretched to domestic policies, and foreign affairs and politics. This new kind of war was also directed towards the 'enemy within', as demonstrated by, but not limited to, excessive censorship and retaliation against citizens by the government, for the expression of political criticism, during the notorious McCarthy era and Stalinism. The Cold War era, which lasted until the fall of the Berlin Wall in 1989, swept the world into an ideological conflict between communism and capitalism as represented by the eastern

European countries in the Soviet bloc and the western European countries allied with the USA. In the middle of this, the media played a catalytic role in the construction of anti-communist propaganda in the West and in defending the actions of the state in the Soviet countries. Divided into two parts (East and West) and four control zones (Russian, American, British and French), walled Berlin was the crudest representation of this segregation.

Only two years after the end of the Second World War, the UN had already expressed concerns about matters of freedom of information. The US media lobby (newspapers and news agencies) supported the idea of a convention on the *individual's* rights of freedom of information and of the inclusion of these rights in the Human Rights Declaration (as discussed in Chapter 3). However, they then decided to support the *institutional* freedom of information – that is, the freedom of the press – instead. This US version of the freedom of expression became the dominant one. It was criticized for, in fact, signalling freedom of expression for a few media monopolies (see Hamelink 1994: 155).

The need for international agreements on fundamental communication issues such as the freedom of information had been recognized by states and media professionals early on but became more acute during the Second World War. The impact of international media increased, although the actual players remained few in number, mainly controlled by the old empires, the USA and the Soviet Union. The VOA, funded by the US government, played an important role during the US military involvement in the Korean War in 1950 and in subsequent anti-communist propaganda. Moscow Radio remained the world's largest single international broadcaster until the mid-1970s, almost as large as all the international US broadcasters put together (VOA, Radio Liberty and Radio Free Europe) (Thussu 2000: 30). The BBC managed to inspire respect among its audiences both nationally and internationally, mainly due to two factors: its style, which made it very distinct from its US counterpart, characterized by British 'understatement', and also the fact that it conveyed a sense of independence, again when compared to other media, which allowed it to criticize the British government even if only indirectly (see Seymour-Ure 1996; Thussu 2000). The BBC World Service created vast audiences in the countries to which it had been transmitting and, for many, it was seen as a reliable source of information. In some cases, the World Service was one of the few information sources from the 'free world', especially in its broadcasts to countries with dictatorial regimes, such as Greece and Spain in the 1960s and 1970s.

In 1954 the BBC's national monopoly came to an end with the introduction of a second network designed to be financed by advertising. The Beveridge Committee (1951) argued that advertising need not harm content quality, in particular since an independent body, the Independent Television Authority (ITA), would regulate it. (See Table 1.1 for details of broadcasting committees and related changes in the British media landscape between 1923 and 1990.) The introduction of commercial television in the 1950s is seen by Curran and Seaton (1997: 163) to be the result of a combination of reasons. Pressure was exercised by the commercial lobby that consisted of theatre management and advertisers. Moreover, Churchill and other important members of the government had no particular interest in defending the BBC. The arrival of commercial television led to a relationship of competition with the BBC rather than of complement. This resulted in the two channels gradually depending upon each other to make decisions regarding programming. For example, news programmes and

Table 1.1: Broadcasting committees and change in the British media landscape, 1923–90

Reports	Year	Main task	Main recommendations	Politics and society (during the decade)
Sykes	1923	• To consider contracts or licences • Possible restrictions on broadcasting	• 'the operation of broadcasting . . . [is such a] national service that should not be allowed to become unrestricted commercial monopoly' • Broadcasting should continue to be financed by licence-fee revenues	Social reforms – welfare state; a British radio broadcast heard in the USA; British arrest (and later release) Gandhi; coal and general strikes in Britain; women's right to vote in 1927; women start smoking in public; cartels develop in Japan; Japanese feminists organize New Women's Association
Crawford	1925	• Assessment of public reaction to radio • Organizational structure	• Parliament should review the BBC's accounts annually • Increase in educational programming • Broadcasting of 'moderate amount of controversial matter'	
Selsdon	1935	• To consider the development of television in terms of technological standards	• Baird and EMI Marconi to operate alternative systems for a London station until one system proves to be the best	Fascist and Nazi regimes in Europe; discussions about the rearmament of Germany; general strike in Britain; Latin American economies grow; growth of welfare state
Ullswater	1936	• Constitution, control and finance of BBC in Britain and the Empire	• Decentralization of programming to regions • BBC should be impartial • BBC should consult political parties in important political matters • Provision of cultural programmes for 'public taste' • No advertising as income revenue	

Table 1.1 continued

Reports	Year	Main task	Main recommendations	Politics and society (during the decade)
Hankey	1945	• Reinstatement of television • Technological standards • Provision for export trade	• Establishment of an advisory committee • London service should be re-established and expand to regions • BBC should seek ways to collaborate with the cinema	Division of Germany into zones of influence; civil war in Greece; Education Act in Britain; US film imports in Europe; communist power in China (1949); first meeting of the United Nations; India and Pakistan gain independence from Britain; South Africa institutionalizes Apartheid
Beveridge	1951	• To consider BBC monopoly and advertising as funding method	• BBC should remain monopoly (the Committee was divided) • Funding should continue to be based on licence fees • Increase in political broadcasting • BBC should develop audience research and feedback • 1955 Broadcasting Act • 1959 Obscenity Act	Conservative Party introduces proposal for commercial channel; Cold War era; first military interventions by superpowers in 'third world' countries; Italian social realism in cinema; Marshall Plan; European Economic Community 1958; civil rights movements in USA
Pilkington	1962	• To advise on services to be provided by BBC and ITA, examine whether new services should be provided by other organizations, propose financial conditions	• Criticizes low quality standards of ITV • Criticizes advertising as manipulative • Provides the ideological background for the award of a new channel to BBC • 1964 Broadcasting Act	Berlin Wall; 'May 68' social movements; protests and strikes in France, Germany, and throughout Europe and the USA; the decade of 'sexual revolution'; the contraceptive pill; first woman in space, 1963; first man on the moon, 1969; dictatorship in Greece; cultural revolution in China; execution of Che Guevara, 1966; beginning of gay rights movement in the USA

Table 1.1 continued

Reports	Year	Main task	Main recommendations	Politics and society (during the decade)
Annan	1977	• To consider the 'future of broadcasting'	• 'to preserve British broadcasting as a public service' • Pluralism in media • Role of new technologies, such as cable, Teletext, VCR • Broadcasting Act 1980 • Channel 4: production by independent companies, C4 subsidiary of IBA	USA invades Cambodia; invasion of Cyprus; Britain takes direct rule of Northern Ireland; Britain joins European Economic Community; students' and workers' protests, strong feminist movements in Europe, the USA and elsewhere; restoration of democracy in Greece; Willy Brandt's **Realpolitik**; mid-1970s TV professionals, academics, trade unionists in TV4 campaign; Margaret Thatcher prime minister in 1979; restructuring of welfare state
Hunt	1982	• Inquiry into cable expansion and broadcasting policy	• Identified four functions in cable (cable provider, cable operator, programme/ service provider, programme-maker) • No need for separation of ownership between cable operator and cable provider • Government/political parties should be excluded from cable ownership • New cable authority	Recession; CNN dominates as the news channel worldwide: Gulf War; Soviet Union breaks up
Peacock	1986	• To review the licence fee method of funding	• Call to 'auction' ITV franchises • 'comfortable duopoly' of public and private broadcasters • Consumer sovereignty as the new ideological argument	

Source: adapted from Briggs 1995; Curran and Seaton 1997; Hutchison 1999a; Article 19; Media History Project; **Der Spiegel** (various issues); World History; broadcasting committee reports (as listed above) documentaries proved popular, while programmes of 'high culture' content, such as opera, did not attract audiences. The channels would look to each other's programming to make sure that they did not lag behind in their own content. What this created, however, was a mechanistic and considerably limiting way of determining content (Smith 1974).

Until the Second World War, the BBC did not provide cultural programming for the working classes. Commercial television intensified a strategy that the BBC had already launched: the specialization of programming into Home, Light and Third services, which would provide current affairs, light and serious productions to different audiences. Nevertheless, it was largely due to the public service broadcaster and to an early understanding of the ideas of universal access that by 1956 almost 98 per cent of Britain was able to receive television. It was also on the traditions and codes of conduct developed by the BBC that the new television relied to create its own programming, at least during its first 20 years. Meanwhile, the film industry, dominated by Hollywood productions full of ideas of the 'American dream', swept post-war Europe. Hollywood films further provided the template for the increased production of populist programmes influenced by the American experience, signalling the beginning of an era of intensive commercialism and cultural imperialism for the screen media.

The commercialization of the broadcast media, as the print media before the war, was indicated by the use of advertising in financing the television operation. The increase in advertising and the development of new forms facilitated by the screen became a matter of concern for politicians and academics. The influence of advertising on individual behaviour was a major issue of debate in the 1960s: during the war, the 'advertisement' of goods emphasized the scarcity of resources and called for reasonable, moderate use. Advertising in the 1960s proclaimed exactly the opposite, promoting a culture of accumulation and consumption. These thoughts were reflected in the Pilkington Report (1962), which addressed a number of crucial dimensions of the organization and content of television in Britain. It openly criticized advertising on television as manipulation and for its effect on programming. Popular entertainment programmes were seen by the Pilkington Committee as providing a false sense of choice to the public (which broadcasters treated as an undifferentiated mass). The Report gave the BBC a channel that would bring equilibrium vis-à-vis the commercially dominated ITV and more power to the ITA to ensure quality programming in the commercial sector. Commercial television in Britain was obliged to include 'serious' programming (one-third of its total broadcasting hours) and was not allowed to accept sponsorship-type advertising until 1988. Furthermore, advertising space was also controlled and, contrary to the American experience, British commercial television had more power over advertisers than expected since, with its expansion into local networks, it was the major medium that could sell their products. The expansion of regional television, the so-called Channel 3, was not motivated by the ideals of public service broadcasting: advertising revenues increased steadily in the 1960s and 1970s, more people owned television sets and it was easier to define target audiences for advertisers when these were predominantly identified through the programmes they consumed. Nevertheless, the *ideals* of 'public service' broadcasting or programming for the public interest significantly influenced the content of ITV networks up until the era of deregulation, as we will see later.

In the late 1960s, social movements were questioning the status quo in Europe and the US through a series of protests, strikes, talks and political activism at grassroots level. Anti-war movements, together with civil liberties movements for the rights of black people, feminist movements and the left-wing intelligentsia changed the way that we look at politics and social life. The sexual revolution and the struggles for equal civil rights for women and black people, and the right of nations to determine their own fates free from the control of superpowers swept the world. The student revolt and general strike in France in May 1968, the student movements in Germany, protests against the Vietnam War, feminist activism, gay liberation and the protests in Prague were all expressions of the politicization of civil society and the demand for social change. The role of television in society had become the object of criticism, not only due to the subjects it covered – such as the casualties of the Vietnam War, which shocked people and contributed to the end of the war – but also in terms of what it did not cover, as in the case of Greece, where television was born during the military dictatorship and was under the total control of the armed forces.

In Britain, the 76 Group, a pressure group composed of academics and programme-makers called for a comprehensive review of the broadcasting structure and financing. This inquiry into the broadcasting system commenced under the Labour government in 1970, but was stopped by the Conservative government elected later that year. In 1971 more pressure came from the Trades Union Congress (TUC) conference, which called for an investigation into the ownership and control of the mass media (Freedman 2001). Throughout the 1970s the academic study of the media in Britain produced a series of critiques and study centres that stimulated the debate on the role of the media. This critical debate was expressed in the Annan Report (1977), where the questions asked by the committee were quite radical compared to the conservative past of media policies. The report addressed the relation of ITV's profits to the quality of service which it provided to the nation. It also addressed the need for accountability on the part of the broadcasters. However, the recommendations were not as radical as the questions asked, the issues involved and the expectations of trade unions and academics. Accountability of, and transparency of, the broadcasters' structure and organization did not increase, and generally the recommendations did not offer any substantial change. The most important achievement of the Annan Report was the establishment of a fourth channel that would not be a second ITV, but rather a channel with educational character.

The 1970s also saw the conglomeration of the media: industrialists and other business people entered the press field, owning several papers in several geographic areas as part of their business portfolio. The Thomson organization was one of them in the 1970s, owning small-town papers and radio stations in Canada and expanding with the purchase of the *Scotsman* (in 1954) and *The Times* (in 1966), and diversifying into the business of North Sea oil (Seymour-Ure 1996: 121). The Pearson company, with interests mainly in the international banking sector and property, bought the *Financial Times* in the 1950s and *The Economist*. Rupert Murdoch bought the *Sun* (in 1969) and launched it as a tabloid; by 1981 he also owned *The Times*.

In 1982, Channel 4 started broadcasting programmes mainly intended to include the work of independent producers, with content catering for neglected audiences. By that time the local radio stations were also covering the majority of the UK population and, under the Thatcher government, restrictions over their ownership were lifted, which led to an increased ownership concentration with almost 30 per cent of all local radio stations belonging to the press by the end of the 1980s. The development of Channel 4, with programmes addressing ethnic and other minorities, and openly discussing controversial issues such as homosexuality, was not appealing to the government. The Conservative government attacked the notion of public service broadcasting and the BBC in particular, in direct and indirect ways throughout its term of office, while it offered support to commercial television and the conglomeration of the press. Thatcher's opinion of the BBC was not positive: she regarded it as a bureaucratic, left-wing, badly managed organization, and she made no effort to conceal her opinion. Indeed the rise of 'new right' politics both in the USA and in Britain in the 1980s created a hostile environment for public service organizations in general. Thatcher systematically encouraged her 'favourite' press mogul, Murdoch, while making sure that a culture of fear and self-censorship dominated the working culture of the BBC, especially when it came to the coverage of current affairs such as the Falklands War and events in Northern Ireland (Eldridge *et al.* 1997). Two examples give a vivid picture of the (repressive) involvement of the Tory government in broadcasting. Mrs Thatcher was not happy with the way that the BBC reported on 'British troops' in the Falklands (as opposed to '*our* troops'), being particularly annoyed by a live phone-in programme, where she received tough questions from the public (Curran and Seaton 1997; Glasgow University Media Group 1982). Another major bone of contention was the coverage of Northern Ireland. The BBC's position was that its commitment to impartial information and objectivity required coverage to be given to Sinn Fein, whereas, according to the Tory government, not all have the right to have a voice – in order to have a voice one would have to change in order to earn such a right (Curran and Seaton 1997).

Murdoch's News Corporation was in favour of the government abandoning the licence fee as a means of financing the BBC and instead introducing advertising revenue for the public service broadcaster. News Corporation was planning to expand into satellite television, and the role of BBC in the domestic market as well as its presence internationally with the World Service were a barrier to these plans. *The Times* and the *Sun* repeatedly attacked the BBC, while their owner was lobbying the government to prepare the road to deregulation. The Peacock Committee (1986) was set up by Thatcher to look into the question of an alternative to the licence fee method of funding for the BBC. The Committee did not think that advertising would be a plausible method of funding for the service delivered by BBC. However, although the public service character of the broadcaster had, at least for the time being, been preserved, internal restructuring and the rise of a managerial culture had begun. Meanwhile, European public service broadcasters were losing ground to incoming private channels and satellite television, neo-liberal politics had already undermined public services and the welfare state, while the fall of the Berlin Wall signalled the 'end of history' for some (Fukuyama 1992) and the triumph of capitalism.

The end of history?

The 1980s witnessed a constant and systematic process of deregulation, mainly driven by industrial lobbies and the rise of neo-liberal politics, which favoured the privatization of public services. Pressure from these groups heralded a decade characterized by the dominance of the commercial model of public communication in British society and throughout Europe. The political attacks on the BBC in Britain by its national government were reinforced by the role of the press in lobbying for the opening of the market to private broadcasting operators. Public service broadcasters (PSBs) in Europe saw their audience shares drop and their *raison d'être* questioned. Most European countries had organized their public service broadcasters around a licence-fee model of financing and some controlled advertising. PSBs also meant state broadcasters, in that the government had direct or indirect control over their production and organizational structure. More often than not, this control extended to decisions regarding content. The collapse of the socialist regimes in eastern Europe deprived public opinion of an alternative proposal to the capitalist system. Up to 1989, the world was divided into two ideological camps. The media played a crucial role in maintaining this ideological division. With the major ideological alternative 'defeated', the American media model, used as a normative justification of the free market, defined the application of new satellite and cable technologies, with the aim of launching new markets for private media. Liberalism was claimed to be the 'winning' ideology: the 'end of history' of ideas was sealed with the domination of the market.

Three parallel developments shaped the character of broadcasting and the media: the multiplication of channels accessible outside national boundaries, the disintegration of state broadcasting and the increase in broadcasting markets (Raboy 1995: 3). It is important to note, however, that the expansion of media markets and the creation of new ones only apply as far as multinational corporations are concerned. Indeed, although the markets expanded to include various media services and methods of transmission – such as broadcasting and narrowcasting, the Internet and the print press – the media owners who benefited from this expansion were limited to a few corporations. The consolidation of markets and the increased pressure on public service broadcasters may indeed have signalled the 'end of history' – an end characterized by the absolute domination of entertainment media content, the tabloidization of the media in general, the decrease in the available information sources and increase in communication media and, finally, the abandonment of the ethics of public service and public interest in favour of the rationale of liberal markets and consumer sovereignty.

FURTHER READING

Arthurs, J. (1994) Women and Television. In Hood, S. (ed.) *Behind the Screens: The Structure of British Television in the Nineties*, London: Lawrence & Wishart.
An important text that directly addresses women's contribution to British media and, in particular, television. Although somewhat dated in its statistical data, the chapter offers a comprehensive overview of the arguments for greater participation of women in the programme-making of the media. It focuses on the representation of women in the media workforce in the 1990s and its impact on content and programming.

Briggs, A. and Burke, P. (2002) *A Social History of the Media: From Gutenberg to the Internet*, London: Polity: Chapter 5 (Processes and Patterns).
A very good comprehensive introduction to the social shaping of communications technology including the railways, mail, telegraph and telephones. It discusses the international dimensions of communications technology and the developments that occurred in other countries. Chapter 5 offers a semi-comparative view of the historical background of communication media and their significance for the military and commerce.

chapter two

Industry and trends

The history of the development of the British media reveals a number of issues that are worth serious consideration, about the media as institutions, as industries and as means of communication. Certainly, statements can be made about the multiplicity of the role that media play in human societies. They provide pathways through which communication takes place and information is disseminated. They can facilitate dialogue among different groups, institutions or countries. They present us with images of the world, of distant places and times. They create culture. The media (as institutions) are dependent on technology. They *are* technologies. The media are industries, and they are important economic factors in modern markets.

Understanding the British media system

The development of the media in Britain points to the effects of technological development (cable, satellite), social change (civil rights, rights of women), economic imperatives (internationalization of capital) and developments in the international community, such as wars. Understanding the factors that shape media systems involves the study of the systems surrounding the media. In particular, the role of ownership and technology should not be underestimated.

In his comparative study of France, the Netherlands, Germany, the Soviet Union and Russian Federation, Browne (1999) examined the media systems by identifying and analysing the factors influential on the nature of each media system. By defining external and internal factors, Browne effectively placed media systems within the context of other 'systems'. These were generic factors, such as geography, demographic/linguistic and cultural characteristics; financing of the media; control and influence; communications policy; the relationship of media with their audiences; and finally programming. This book loosely follows the main idea that a sufficient identification of the media system requires us to take into account the broader environment within which the media operate. The immediate factors affecting the nature of the media can be found within the boundaries of the nation-state since this is the immediate point of reference for domestic consumers.

Cultural familiarity, or *proximity*, between media products and their consumers is quite important for making sense of, and therefore consuming, programming, texts or music. Audiences interpret the media goods within the cultural and social contexts in which they live. This means that different interpretations of the same product are possible not only among audiences in very diverse sociocultural settings, such as different countries, but also among people within the same national space. At the same time, however, the possibility of even beginning to process information and interpret it in terms of concepts and ideas presupposes a knowledge base that will allow this process to take place. Unless, for example, we know what the term 'newspaper' stands for, what the role of a newspaper can be or what we should expect from a situation comedy, we cannot make sense of the product we are dealing with. We need the words, the concepts and an agreed convention on which we can base our interpretative process: we need language.

Language can take different forms and is not limited to the spoken or written word. Language is formed from the arrangements of national symbols, visual material, architectural planning, and so forth. In this respect, language represents knowledges and ways we make sense of the world. To use media (whether press, broadcasting or Internet) we need to be able to understand the conventions of the medium in question and interpret the arrangements of words, texts and images. It is therefore important that we not only understand the linguistic conventions of the medium (language, idiom, etc.) but also the conventions of the consumed text that are associated with its genre. Furthermore, as audiences, we need to be able to understand the particularities and cultural references of the content of the text. It is perhaps this difficulty, the specific cultural references, that makes some media texts more difficult to 'export' to other cultures. With the increasing exchange of cultural products, however, and in particular with the increasing export of US films, television series, music and news, together with the internationalization of the English language, younger generations in particular derive pleasure from these products. What is perhaps interesting is that for those generations that grow up with global media and their products, such as MTV, *Sex and the City* and Madonna, 'American' culture can be seen as part of one's own culture. In this global setting, Britain is the second most powerful media exporter in the world, second only to the USA (Tunstall and Machin 1999). But what are the factors that define Britain's media as one of the few leaders internationally, and how do British media form their 'identity' for their own domestic audiences?

Britain is a culturally diverse society, whose citizens can place their ethnic origins in Asia, Australia, Europe and the Americas. Indian and Pakistani communities are strongly represented, as are the Chinese, black Caribbean, Cypriot and other diasporas. Britain is also home to many people who are 'foreign' citizens – that is, citizens of other nations but who live and work in Great Britain. These people may be citizens of other EU countries, for example, and are an integral part of British society. At the same time, the UK consists of administrative regions that to an extent make up different nations, with only few of the characteristics of statehood. It is perhaps Scotland that has the strongest presence as a region with its own political system, since Devolution in 1999, Wales is asserting its right to self-governance in matters of education, among other areas, and Northern Ireland has its power sharing executive. England remains the decision-making centre in many ways and continues to present a centralized form of governance, industrial development and cultural dominance over media. It is no coincidence that the world's biggest media and Britain's own have at least an office, if not headquarters, in London. The City of London is the epicentre of stock market and banking activity, and the seat of the British government. Furthermore, southern England is home to extensive military constructions and training fields.

Regionality in Britain has been reflected and reproduced in the organization of the media system. Television and radio stations offer locally or regionally directed content, and programming makes use of the particularities of the regions, tending to address 'local' news stories, and make use of accents and dialects in fiction programmes. Newspapers tend to emphasize the particular locality alongside news from the 'centre' or international affairs. Some programmes are addressed to the perceived interests of minorities.

The fact that Britain is an English-speaking country – although idiom, minority languages and dialects play an important role in the construction of cultural identities in the country – is a great advantage for media production and revenue. It is to the establishment of Great Britain as a media power during the First and particularly the Second World War that the English language owes its founding as, effectively, *the* international language, despite the fact that Chinese and Spanish are probably the most widely spoken languages on the planet. Britain's colonialism played an important role in establishing the dominance of the English language. English was the official administrative language of the colonies, while in the post-colonial era, it continues to be the language of elites. The dominance of Britain in international communications has been aided by a dynamic, even aggressive, development of communication media (the founding of the BBC) that played a catalytic role in the Second World War, as discussed in Chapter 1. This linguistic dominance has been further established through the dominance of American content on the world's screens, be they cinema, television or computer (via the Internet). The production of English-speaking programmes is aided by the availability of markets such as Australia, New Zealand, the USA, and the Commonwealth countries and former British colonies. In such places, this language is still spoken by educated elites or has become the official language of the nation. The existence and further cultivation of these 'ready-made' markets offer a good starting point for media exports, especially audiovisual programming and books.

The early twenty-first century exemplifies a set of changes in the production, ownership and even consumption of media texts, whose developing stages we can trace back to the 1980s and right through the 1990s. The processes of deregulation and reregulation (which is discussed in more detail in later chapters) have facilitated the complete commercialization of the broadcasting spectrum, even in countries ideologically subscribed to media monopoly. Such media systems were those under Soviet rule, where the state had tight control over media outcomes. In the countries of the former Soviet Union the role of journalism and the press was considered to be the education of the workers in the principles of communism and the building of the workers' state. In the West, the official national television and radio channels were more often than not accused of being controlled by the government, especially during the Cold War. State monopoly over broadcasting was, rather, the rule in Europe and in most countries in the world. For western capitalism, the ideological positions of mainstream media fulfilled a role dictated by a Cold War climate characterized by anti-communist, pro-capitalist ideologies. Public service broadcasters in Europe are products of interwar periods.

But, most significantly, the BBC has managed to become the ultimate point of reference, the leading example, the defining institution not only of the British Empire and the Great Empire later on – it has also become the 'symbol' of the institution of public service broadcasting in Europe. It has in addition developed an unsurpassable reputation for objectivity and accuracy among international audiences, through its radio news programmes, reaching audiences from Europe to the Americas and China. The BBC has become the epitome of British media not just for British people living in Britain, but also for international audiences and citizens of other countries living in Britain.

The effects of deregulation across Europe have created a number of problems for public service broadcasters and the BBC has often been accused of either leaning too close to the government or of being too critical of the government. It has been accused of wasting tax payers' and licence fee payers' money by commissioning obscure programmes that attract only small audiences. Like all PSBs in Europe, the BBC has been accused of bureaucracy and inflexibility; it has even been attacked on grounds of 'legitimacy', whereby its *raison d'être* has been questioned. The new culture of pay-per-view and subscription to broadcasting services, as orchestrated by the telecommunication and media companies to secure revenues, is based on the assumption that texts and programmes are services for which one should pay. Consumer sovereignty over citizenship has become the trademark of the era of commercialization of the media. In this respect audiences should not be obliged to pay a licence fee for programmes they do not consume. This crisis in the acceptance of the BBC has meant that the very scope and role of the institution have had to be re-examined.

As discussed in Chapters 3 and 4, on policy, the fight to protect PSBs has become an international one, with debates and policy-making taking place at a European and global level. Considering the immense powers of transnational corporations to exercise pressure on politicians and policy-makers, it is not hard to imagine that our era is one characterized by a 'clash of the titans'. On the one hand, we have the symbols of public ownership and public service, on the other, the forces of the 'free' market. The ideological battles fought over control of the airwaves and broadcast spectrum reflect the very real and (material) struggle for the domination of media systems that have quite different interests at heart.

Ownership patterns of the British media

Globalization has brought changes to the ownership patterns of the media in most countries in the world. These patterns change very often and this makes it difficult to map them against a stable framework, however, it is safe to say that the tendency seems to be further concentration of ownership and increased business linkages among rivals. Most media are connected with each other in unexpected or indirect ways, with rival companies having shares in the same company; similarly, pornographic media are directly linked with mainstream media through such patterns of ownership and distribution.

One of the core characteristics of contemporary media ownership is its transnational base. Companies based in countries other than Britain own British media, which begs the question of how 'British' the British media are. In some cases, such as that of the BBC, it is not difficult to identify the 'Britishness' of the medium, built upon the history of the policies that shaped the BBC but also its relationship with audiences in Britain *and* abroad. Certain forms of media content appear to be particularly British: *Coronation Street*, say, *EastEnders* or perhaps page three of the *Sun*. Looking at the ownership of what we call British media we can see that, of the top five most successful British publishers in terms of copies sold, three belong to German transnationals, one is based in the USA and one is British.

More specifically, Transworld, the number one publishing house with total sales of over 6 million copies in 1998, as well as Random House, the fourth in terms of sales, belong to Bertelsmann AG, the German multi/transnational media company; HarperCollins, the second in terms of sales, belongs to News International, which belongs to News Corporation owned by modern press lord Rupert Murdoch and his media empire. Only Hodder Headline was a British company in 1999 (Stokes 1999: 13). Yet, currently, the UK's book publishing companies are among the most powerful and profitable industries in the world. Books published by British publishing houses are directly exported to Australia and the USA and, very often, are also published by the American branches of British companies (Tunstall and Machin 1999). This is particularly the case in academic publishing. The book market is so important that companies actively pursue the publication of topics that address some aspect that is relevant to US readers. The obvious reason is, of course, to produce cultural artefacts that are familiar in form and content to American audiences and therefore expand sales to wider English-speaking markets around the world. The same tactic is followed in the film industry. One of the most successful British films in recent history was 1994's *Four Weddings and a Funeral*. The film was supported financially by the European Union under the MEDIA programme and enjoyed some success in the USA (European films are rarely shown in US film theatres). The inclusion of an American actress (Andy McDowell) proved a good recipe for success – a recipe followed in the production of *Notting Hill* and other British films, or films made in Hollywood featuring British actors and actresses, with the aim of capitalizing on the respective markets.

These examples do not even begin to describe the increasing importance international markets have attained in the era of globalization. Media products and services depend on ever expanding markets to make a profit. Tunstall and Machin (1999: 133) note that British and German markets are seen as indicative of the degree of acceptance and success of Hollywood films. In 2001, of the top 20 box office hits worldwide, 19 were US productions. Of these 19 films only two were co-productions, with Great Britain (*Bridget Jones's Diary*) and New Zealand (*Lord of the Rings*). The only non-US film listed among the top 20 was a Japanese production, *Spirited Away* (Focus 2002: 9). The same year, the USA released 462 films, while the European Union produced 625. Yet, 65.4 per cent of cinema admissions were for US films; of the remainder, 7.5 per cent were for British films. In Germany, 17 out of 20 top listed films were US productions; in the UK, just one film in the top 20 was a production that did not involve the USA as a co-producer: *The Others* was a Spanish production with Nicole Kidman playing the main protagonist in the film (Focus 2002). Of the six co-productions, Great Britain was present in three, on the same list (Focus 2002).

If we take the dominance of Hollywood over other national or regional cultural goods as

Table 2.1: Numbers and origins of films showing on prime-time TV during week 13–19 April 2002, on channels viewed in Switzerland, Germany and Austria

Country of production	Saturday	Sunday	Monday	Tuesday	Wednesday	Thursday	Friday
USA	10	11	3	4	6	4	10
D	8	3	8	3	5	5	2 (ARD)
GB	1 (WDR)	1 (ZDF)	1	1 (HR)	0	0	0
CH	1 (ARTE)*	0	0	0	0	0	0
A	0	1 (ARD)	0	0	0	1 (BR)	0
European & European co-productions	F: 1 (ORB) D/IT:1 (NDR) E/F:1 (HR)	F: 1 (SFB1) F: 1 (NDR) D/A: 1 (MDR)	F/IT: 1 (ARTE)	F:1 A/D: 1 (3SAT) IT/GB: 1 (SFB1) D/IT: 1 (NDR)	F: 1 (WDR)	D/ZA: 1 IT/F: 1 (3SAT) ISL/Nor/S/D: 1 (ARTE)	F: 1 (ARTE) USA/GB: 1
World	USA/HK:1	0	HU:1 (3 SAT) Japan: 1 (MDR)		USA/CAN: 1	0	RU: 1 (3SAT) USA/AUS: 1
total	24	19	15	12	13	13	16

1. The letters in brackets denote the public service broadcasters showing the films.
2. D = Germany; A = Austria; GB = Great Britain; CH = Switzerland; I = Italy; E = Spain; F = France; HU = Hungary; CAN = Canada; ZA = South Africa; HK = Hong Kong; N = Norway; S = Sweden; ISL = Iceland; AUS = Australia; RU = Russia.
3. Of the 72 top films in the four weeks as listed by TV Vier magazine (Switzerland), US films = 46 (58 per cent of all proposed 'top films'); European = 20 (of which none are Swiss productions, 10 are from Germany and 4 from the UK) and 3 are D/US productions (approx. 28 per cent); other = 3 (2 from Canada and 1 from Australia).
* ARTE is a German/French public service broadcasting project, transmitting in two languages, also available to all these countries. Channels are available to predominantly German-speaking audiences (Germany, Austria, German-speaking Switzerland). All the above channels broadcast to all three countries and are accessible without cable or other subscription.

an example, one of the most striking differences is the budget available for the production of films. The average cost of producing a feature film in the USA is nearly US$50 million, while it is a mere US$8 million for a British production (Focus 2002: 7). One must remember, though, that the cost of British productions is among the highest in the EU. This obscene difference indicates a number of conditions that can determine the very nature of the product as well as its economic viability. For one thing, higher budgets allow the purchase of better equipment, there is more time available for the production process and therefore an end-product that is technically superior to other products that may lack the same resources. At the same time, such films are able to cover their costs – and make a profit – through their distribution to large-scale markets: first, the domestic market (the USA) and, second, world markets. Distribution is therefore the next vital arm of the production–consumption process. Hollywood can also afford *not* to cover its costs or make a profit as long as the products are otherwise acknowledged through awards and press coverage, and they help maintain the ideological 'aura' of American culture.

We should not forget that film-making companies are part of huge conglomerates involved in a series of activities, able to support and distribute their films throughout the world. Tunstall and Machin (1999: 131) focus on the reluctance of the British to design a specific export policy for the lack of success of the British film industry in selling its wares to Hollywood. As the authors put it, a defensive Britain, focused on 'parochial . . . caricatured, British idiosyncrasy and eccentricity', means that films produced in Britain have too many (British) cultural references for American audiences to understand and/or identify with.

A similar argument can be made for television series production. Tunstall and Machin again identify a problem with Britain's approach to television fiction in terms of short series (six to seven episodes). The problem with this production planning is that it does not fit American standards, where networks look for massive productions that will fill thousands of hours of programming. As can be seen, then, the British – or indeed European – approach (since similar patterns can be found in other European countries) is rooted in the very nature of the European broadcasting system, one that until recently was driven mainly by content rather than quantity of programme hours. At the same time, television programmes are often very close to the 'local' culture, expressing (and reiterating) culture-specific meanings, texts and images. To the 'untrained' eye of the American viewer, these references may appear irrelevant, incomprehensible or unacceptable. Think, for example, of the reaction of US media and audiences to Ali G's sarcastic (British?) humour when he 'confused' 7-11 (a chain store) with 9/11 (the terrorist attacks in New York) in the performer's US-addressed programme (besides the importance of cultural familiarity, the example of Ali G making a programme for the US market also demonstrates the importance placed upon the winning of the American audience markets). Here we may find that cultural or national stereotypes work better, in commercial terms, than attempts at realistic depiction of aspects of social and cultural life.

Let us consider the case of *Inspector Morse* (ITV) as an example of a TV series that has been particularly successful in the UK and abroad. We will find that the content corresponds more closely to the dominant, fairly stereotypical, impressions of what it means to be British. 'Britishness' is a synonym for 'Englishness' to international audiences. London, red telephone boxes, red double-decker buses, teapots, umbrellas, the Union Jack, golf and – of course – the BBC are 'British' things. England still remains most vivid in popular culture and imagination as the epitome of 'island identity'. In particular, southern England is often promoted as representative of British national identity to 'Others' abroad. In order for a cultural product to achieve this, it has to draw on mechanisms of constructing its own internal or domestic 'Others'. *Inspector Morse* and other similar series, such as *Midsomer Murders* also produced by ITV, play with preconceptions of what means to be British. The picturesque little towns and villages spread around the countryside become locations where intrigue and murder encroach. Inspector Morse (or Barnaby in *Midsomer Murders*) are presented as *bon viveurs*: ale-lover Morse and wine connoisseur Barnaby listen to classical music (or go to Shakespearean performances), appreciate high arts, have had a classical education, think deeply about the human condition, preserve a gentleman's code of conduct in their mannerisms and, of course, drive British cars. Both characters are accompanied by detectives, assistants who represent the uncivilized, primitive, uncultivated, simple soul of the lower classes, the men who aspire to become – but we know they can never be – fine English gentlemen. *Inspector Morse's* appeal stretches to four continents: the series is broadcast in Australia, Belgium, Canada, Eire, Holland, New Zealand, Mexico, South Africa and the USA. Another series, also true to the mystery/crime-solving genre, *A Touch of Frost*, is less successful with international audiences. The scene is set in the north of England. Here, there are few hanging baskets dangling beside the prettily mullioned windows of picturesque cottages, there are no landscaped gardens, and hardly any scenes are shot during the spring. The backdrop to the action is grey, rainy and cold. The investigation scenes are located in rundown housing estates, windblown streets, bridges and warehouses, and shabby, grey and impersonal police offices and interrogation rooms. This is the location of formerly industrial England, where the working classes are now transformed into masses of unemployed or casual workers, where youth suffocates under severe cuts on public services and education budgets. Poverty, discrimination and deprived communities are represented in this fictional programme not in a nostalgic or romantic light, but under the harsh spotlight of hard reality. Inspector Frost is a man who believes in justice, and is fed up with bureaucracy and the increased red tape that constantly prevents him from getting on with his real job (finding criminals and bringing them to justice). He is an honest, working-class man who expresses his thoughts in a direct and straightforward manner; his is not the way of an English gentleman. He is a sensitive, fair, tyrannized by his superior, an inspector who knows life's roughness. The specific cultural references to the conditions of living in industrial England are hard for 'Others' to consume. For one thing, the places where the series is shot do not necessarily feature in tourist brochures. Frost is seen eating unhealthy white-bread toasted sandwiches, drinking greasy tea in the colourless staff canteen or cheap beer at the corner pub. He has a strong working-class accent and buys his clothes at Oxfam. This unglamorous, unsophisticated life finds it difficult to attract high ratings among audiences that have been trained to watch the rich endlessly plotting their new romance/company scam in the American soaps. The realist undertones of the series tend to express the greyer, non-cosmopolitan side of Britishness.

When examining the conditions under which certain programmes become commercial successes in other markets, mostly defined in terms of national territories, it is important to

Table 2.2: Randomly selected television weeks: films shown during prime-time TV (20.00–24.00 hrs)

Films on TV	Broadcasting Country			
Country of production	UK (14–20 April 2002)	FINLAND (18- 24 January 2002)	GREECE (13–19 April 2002)	GERMANY, SWITZERLAND, AUSTRIA (13–19 April 2002)
USA	14	6 (all on MTV3, TV4 commercial)	29 (all on commercial)	48
UK	2 (Scottish ITV)	2	2 (1: ET1 public)	4 (3 on public channels)
Domestic		1 (YLE public)	12 (1: ET1 public)	34 German (2 ARD public) 1 Swiss (ARTE public) 2 Austrian (BR; ARD public)
Other European	0	0	1 (German)	17 (various; 16 on public channels 1 USA/UK on commercial)
World	0	0		6 various (4 on public channels)
Total	16	9	44	112

Source: data collected from Tilerama (GR), Scotland on Sunday (UK), TV-Today (D), TV-Vier (CH)

take into account the ways in which texts offer themselves as objects of easy-reading, unproblematic consumption and cultural proximity. This should not be understood as an all-encompassing justification for the failure of poor works. However, the degree to which televisual or other texts attempt to challenge stereotypes or base their success on exploiting unjustified perceptions can be a factor that is difficult to ignore.

Transatlantic commercial success can be achieved if the programmes produced offer a style that can easily be adapted, by changing the textual arrangement of the product (dialogues, topics, locations) to suit the (mainstream) local cultural standards. One such example is the quiz show *Who Wants to Be a Millionaire?* (ITV). The idea – contestants answer trivia questions and win a monetary prize depending on the number of correct answers – is in accordance with a number of almost universally understood values. These belong to the ideology that makes acceptable the logic of 'earning money' and being rewarded for certain kinds of knowledge and for risk-taking (when the contestants have to make a decision to 'gamble' and proceed with the game or take whatever money they have won). Such game shows operate at the level of lowest common denominator, and a careful analysis of their content reveals that they are more likely to reward conventional knowledge and therefore validate the reward system of western societies based on the idea of merit but constructed according to mainstream – dominant – values. The show has been adapted for viewing in many countries throughout the world, as has the 'reality' show *Pop Idol* (and other similar programmes). Again, these shows cultivate preconceived ideas about merit (talent and skills) and the (American/capitalist) dream of 'making it big' and the glamorous world of the media.

Despite the considerable success of programmes produced in the UK, among which are documentaries made by the BBC, it is generally the case that 'difficult' material, experimental films, or independent and highly controversial productions do not offer themselves as material that seeks to be financed and distributed by transnational mainstream media. Small, independent media producers and film-makers depend on raising funds from private sources, and on funds from the state or other friendly media, such as Channel 4. In addition, it is equally important that there are no film-making 'moguls' in Britain, at least none of the enormity of those to be found in Hollywood. The British film industry depends on sales in the UK to cover costs but even when these sales are made, it is not certain that they will create profit that can be re-invested in making more films. Distribution channels, movie theatres and screens are very important to the economic success of a film. In the 1990s, the most successful British productions were distributed by Miramax (owned by Disney), Fox (owned by NewsCorp) or Polygram (owned by Philips) (Tunstall and Machin 1999: 132). At the same time, US exhibitors occupy the largest part of movie theatres in the UK, while non-US cinema chains have established links with US companies and show their productions (Hill 1999: 82).

In 1998, the five most prominent film distributors in the UK were Fox, Buena Vista, UIP, Warner and Columbia Tri-Star; these owned over 77 per cent of market share (*Screen Digest* 1999: 48). A comparative look at the programmes of some European countries around the same period reveals two things: Europeans watch US films and sometimes British ones. European audiences do not watch European films other than domestic productions in their own language (see Tables 2.1 and 2.2).

This case offers a good example of the underlying problems associated with cultural production and consumption. Most significantly, the assumption that national media markets can operate away from the factors that influence global trade is parochial. Similarly, ideas about the 'purity' of national culture or the role of national industries need to be attuned to the impact of the forces associated with globalization. The internationalization of trade, the opening up of (trade) borders and the technologies that allow a virtual time–space continuum almost independent of the limitations of physical time and space, facilitate a non-stop, round-the-clock, worldwide commercial exchange and banking activity. In other words, capital never sleeps. Around the world, people use mass media for very different purposes at different times of day. However, at any given moment someone somewhere is consuming the media for some purpose. The internationalization of media, both as industries and as products, is creating a web of interwoven images, texts, messages, sounds, bearing with them the social conditions of their production, and further setting and exploiting the modes of their consumption. In very specific ways, the internationalization of the media can be observed at three important levels of the 'life cycle' of the media: media production, media ownership and media consumption. These levels are not meant to be understood as chronological stages. The production and consumption of media and cultural goods do not stop; often production and consumption take place at the same time as is the case with 'reality TV' or live shows.

Equally important are the patterns of ownership of the media. These cannot be considered fixed. To describe the fluidity of media ownership, not only in terms of *who* owns the media but also *what* media, becomes a difficult and almost mundane task. The media industry changes hands in the same way football clubs change players (I owe this parallelism to Andrew Beck). The most prominent features of this economic activity are mergers and acquisitions. Companies buy branches or shares in other companies, gaining access to national markets or simply expanding into already existing ones. One of the immediate effects of this is the creation of media oligopolies. Cross-ownership is a not rare phenomenon. Companies of different media and services extend from newspapers to news agencies and production companies, but also integrate vertically to contain as many stages of production and distribution as possible.

On the one hand, globalization is often discussed as the free, timeless/borderless interaction between peoples, nations and markets. It is, however, important to consider that aspects of this interaction are controlled and managed in indirect but efficient ways. These involve aspects of the economic or market behaviour of consumers. Although it is also true that consumers have a certain power to direct the market – for example, by complaining about inappropriate/offensive content or by becoming ecologically aware or supporting fair trade – it is also true that companies manage the demands made by the public in a profitable way. Most importantly, however, big companies want to minimize uncertainty in the market. One of the most effective ways of exercising control over the market is by managing public discourse (Macdonald 2003). This means that companies need to control what is said and written publicly about their products. The best way to do this is by owning the media and by managing the content of media they do not own through the systematic use of marketing strategies and public relations. Marketing strategies aim to direct consuming habits, and therefore the expenditure of money and fiscal assets, towards new products. Company strategies have three overarching aims: the creation of new needs that the company's new products will cover; to maintain the company's public image in accordance with its financial goals; and to maintain the company's positive public profile by managing crisis situations. The media world is no different in this respect. Media companies make sure their products receive (mostly) good press, and are promoted through events and communications that target the customer. *Matrix Reloaded*, for example, was promoted worldwide by websites, radio and television commercials, magazines and film-news programmes and, of course, via trailers in cinemas. However, the film was not just promoted in terms of it being a new movie. A vast amount of ink (or number of bytes) was expended on describing the sunglasses worn by its characters, the clothes, martial arts moves, the music and other film by-products or merchandise. It will be advertised again when it is released on video and DVD, and when it becomes available on pay-per-view from Front Row and other similar services around the world. Vertical integration, leading to cross- and multi-ownership that covers production, distribution and promotion, has become very important in today's world.

Figure 2.1 is a simplified representation of British media ownership patterns and their links to international media conglomerates. The chart shows ownership links where companies own whole companies or parts of companies (percentage of shares) in Britain and in other parts of the world. Ownership patterns are quite complex and difficult to map, not least because they can change rapidly. Our exploration into the labyrinth of transnational media and their relationship with the British media is best served if we start with the most important media institution in Britain: the BBC. The BBC is the largest and oldest UK broadcaster. The corporation runs over 40 local radio stations, an increasing number of digital and cable channels, five national radio stations and through its international arm, BBC Worldwide Ltd, has expanded its activities into the commercial sector. For example, the BBC has joint ventures with UKTV, an umbrella organization of channels, where Pearson TV and Foxtel, Australia are also involved, and the Discovery Channel. Pearson is partly owned by Bertelsmann AG and Foxtel belongs to News Corporation (a subsidiary of News International).

To international audiences, the BBC has mostly been known through its radio news programmes as these are broadcast through the BBC World Service. BBC Digital is carried by cable operators (ntl and Telewest, the biggest cable companies in Britain) as are the Independent Television (ITV) network (mainly owned by Granada and Carlton) and Five (formerly Channel 5), which is owned by RTL, a subsidiary of the German Bertelsmann AG, the largest publishing company in the world. Telewest, the cable operator, is owned by TCI, which was bought out by the American telecommunications giant AT&T in 2002. TCI also owns 20 per cent of Scottish TV as well as the adult channel Playboy, distributed in the UK by ntl and Telewest. AT&T owns 10 per cent of Turner Broadcasting, the owner of CNN, part of the world's biggest media company: America's AOL Time Warner. Furthermore, IPC Media, the company that owns 80 per cent of Britain's magazines, with magazines in its portfolio such as *Loaded*, *Marie Claire* and the *NME*, is itself also owned by AOL Time Warner. The conglomerate owns a number of new media platforms and Internet applications and ISPs such as Netscape Communicator, ICQ messenger and America On-line, alongside its British subsidies of Netscape UK, AOL UK, and so on.

Cross-ownership of the media has proved to be the favourite strategy of transnational companies. As discussed, the activities of media conglomerates expand to all media, involving not only ownership of channels but also acquisition of the press and magazines, cable broadcasting, distribution companies, movie theatres, radio stations and Internet content sites, as well as hardware (computers and cable infrastructure) and software (computer and multimedia programmes). AT&T and News International hold shares in Channel V (Australia), as does the British-owned EMI. Both AOL Time Warner and AT&T (through TCI) are investors in Microsoft. General Electric, a company (or rather a giant) that specializes in, among other things, military aircraft engines, is partners with Microsoft in Intertainer.com, one of the first and biggest programme providers (films and music) direct to PC. AOL Time Warner shares ownership of UCI movie theatres with Walt Disney. The

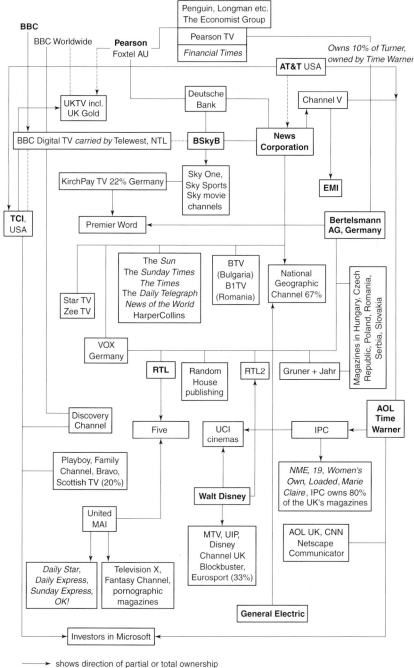

Figure 2.1 British and transnational media ownership patters

Sources: The European Federation of Journalists 2003; Transnationale.org 2003; Underwood 2003; MediaChannel 2002; Guardian Media Guide 2002, Freedomfiles.org 2003

Disney Channel UK, the video rental chain Blockbuster, the movie theatres and distribution company UIP (United International Pictures), all MTV channels and 33 per cent of Eurosport are owned by Walt Disney. Walt Disney shares ownership of RTL-2 with Bertelsmann, which owns publisher Random House and the radio station Atlantic 252 in Britain. Bertelsmann AG also owns Lycos (and Lycos UK). UIP, with films like *Tomb Raider* and the *American Pie* trilogy, and the MTV network are also partly owned by Viacom. Viacom also partly owns Blockbuster and the UK franchise Blockbuster UK, the world's largest video/DVD renter.

It becomes obvious the world's largest media companies are AOL Time Warner, the Walt Disney Company, Bertelsmann AG, Viacom, News Corporation and Vivendi Universal. All of these companies are related, directly or indirectly, to each other. They control the world's media and are shareholders or directly own most of the broadcasting media in Great Britain. Indirectly they are involved in telecommunications, new media, software, programmes, films, radio and the press and, in particular, in services available via cable or satellite.

Channel 4 is financed by advertising, so strictly speaking it belongs to the private sector, however, its mission is to cater for minority interests. Channel 4 has developed its own digital channels, available on subscription, that specialize in entertainment (mainly reality shows, the best-known brand being *Big Brother*, an idea 'imported' from the Netherlands, and US sitcoms) and world cinema. Channel 4 has contributed to the production of many worthy films, drawing on its rich experience in investing in young film-makers. It has launched its own digital services, such as World Cinema and Film Four, which are thought to expand its public service mission of high-quality, innovative programming. At the same time, following the strategy of gigantic media corporations such as Paramount, owned by Viacom (the film-making company that launched its own channels, among which Paramount Comedy exclusively runs Paramount productions), Channel 4 has launched E4, a subsidiary channel consisting of reality TV and mainly US-produced, commercially popular series. Channel 4's digital services are carried by the cable operators ntl, Telewest and on satellite TV via BSkyB.

BSkyB, owned by Murdoch's News International, dominates the British satellite broadcasting network. Deutsche Bank, a powerful German bank involved in a range of other activities such as military industry, is a shareholder in BSkyB, which owns channels such as Sky One, a number of Premier movie channels and Sky Sports. As noted elsewhere in this book, News International (part of News Corporation, the parent company) owns the British newspapers the *Sun*, *The Times* and *The Sunday Times*, the *Daily Telegraph*, *News of the World* and the publishing house HarperCollins.

However, the concentration of ownership of the British media is not so different from international patterns of ownership. British companies have progressed to the acquisition of a large number of media outlets. One of the major media companies is the Daily Mail and General Trust (DMGT), which has the *Daily Mail*, *Mail on Sunday* and 20 per cent of ITN among 21 national and regional newspapers including *Metro* and 27 free local newspapers, 6 television channels, 40 per cent of Teletext, 5 per cent of Classic FM and over one-third of Reuters in its lists. Another powerful media group is United MAI, which publishes the newspapers the *Daily Star*, *Daily Express* and *Sunday Express*, and owns just under 30 per cent of Five. The company also owns a portfolio of pornographic magazines and the channels

Television X and Fantasy Channel, carried by ntl, Telewest and BSkyB, alongside their on-line services. (The pornography industry and its links with the 'mainstream' media are discussed in detail in Chapter 7.)

The structure of the British media industry illustrates the complexity of contemporary communication systems that rely on the interweaving of services, hardware, telecommunications, corporate organization and technical skills to operate technology, but also use it for the consumption of the cultural goods it distributes. In particular, the British media industry is an internationally significant power in areas such as news agencies (the world's largest (Reuters TV and Associated Press TV) are based in London) in its advertising industry and in its geographical–political importance as a location in which media and communication companies can base their European headquarters. The fact that Europe is one of the major economic and political hegemonies of the world makes it imperative for international communication companies to stay abreast of the developments in the continent. Also, the European markets have become extremely profitable for those who can access them. The British and American (US) media industries have 'merged' and now operate together on both sides of the Atlantic – for example, in the book publishing and popular music industries (Tunstall and Machin 1999).

The dynamic relationship of media industries and the state

There are many examples, simple and more sophisticated, through which we can understand the dynamic relationship between the state and the media. The most immediate example is that of the centrality of 'communication officers' and 'spin doctors' in the government's activities. The British press has devoted a significant amount of time and space to coverage of Blair's 'spin doctors', professional media relations people who are seen to be as important to the image of the party and the government as the policies themselves. The *Guardian*, for example, gave extensive coverage to the resignation of government communications director Alastair Campbell (1 and 2 September 2003). The importance of the role of the media in the political life of a country is also indisputable. Blair's first trip as Prime Minister was to pay a visit to Rupert Murdoch; allegations that Tony Blair spoke to Romano Prodi, Italy's then Prime Minister, on 'behalf' of Murdoch show that these two actors – media and state – cannot have a neutral relationship. A visit by the United MAI owner to Downing Street also attracted the attention of the media. This relationship matters because of the power of the media to shape public opinion. At least this is what governments and companies believe, even if some theories tend to pay more attention to the power of subjectivities of the audiences. Media owners effect editorial decisions, and the position the press takes in matters managed by the government can be very influential. The prime example in modern European history is, perhaps, the case of Italy, where Silvio Berlusconi, the country's current Prime Minister and long-time media mogul, used his own media, which 'own' 40 per cent of Italian audiences, to win the election. He did not win the election because people are incapable of thinking for themselves, but because he was able to control the agenda of issues discussed in the media in the pre-election period, and had limitless space and airtime to respond to possible criticisms or silence others. This enabled him to win over those people who were previously 'undecided' (Doyle 2002: 20).

The relationship between governments and media moguls can also be seen in a series of 'favour' exchanges. At the start of the satellite era in Britain, in the early 1980s, the Tory government fostered a UK-directed satellite service. Murdoch's BSkyB was launched and although it is not owned by a British media company, it is nevertheless based in the UK. The government developed its satellite policy in a way that would help the already established BSkyB control the market, while it used this development to provide the rationale for its policy (Goodwin 1998: 121). News Corporation, it must be remembered, is 14th in the top 100 transnational corporations, alongside companies such as BP, Thompson Corporation (another media – publishing – company), Nestlé and Nippon Oil (Japan), although it ranks higher than BP, Coca-Cola, McDonald's and Honda, in their transnationality index. Although it has 70 per cent of its employees in different countries, it still remains a national (Australian) company, 40 per cent of whose assets and 30 per cent of employees are to be found in Australia. This shows that the myth that transnational companies are 'placeless' or truly 'global' companies is not based on quantitative data but rather on ideological fiction (Dicken 2003: 220–7). Despite the fact that the company has subsidiaries in many countries around the world, it is still a fact that decisions are made and assets kept predominantly within the national context of its ownership (Dicken 2003).

In his study of transnational oganizations and the global economy, Dicken includes communications in his discussion of the centrality of the role of distribution companies. We have also seen the importance of distribution systems for media products. Most characteristically, the role of distribution networks and systems defines the extent to which a film will be shown not only within a specific country but also around the world. The US-led deregulation of telecommunications and air transportation industries has swept Europe, even the countries most reluctant or opposed to this, such as France. Air transportation has, among other factors, had an important effect on media hardware, for example, while telecommunications define the digital world of communication today. It is also important to take into account that although the industries pressurize for deregulation, and therefore less control over safety or quality, they lobby for specific 'restrictions' on other non-national companies. This is the case today with the air transportation companies that are not allowed to fly beyond points of entrance in several countries, determining in this way the extent to which courier and postal companies can organize their cargo hubs. In the Chapters 3 and 4, on policy, we will discuss the ideological assumptions and effects of the wave of deregulation accompanied by the process of privatization of publicly owned companies, including those involved in telecommunications and media.

Why do governments seem to be so interested in media and why is it that 'foreign' ownership does not bother national governments, such as the British one, for example? The relationship between state and media is a complex one. On the one hand it can be argued that it is a relationship between state and corporations, as this aspect of the link between communications and the media has intensified in the last two decades. On the other hand, given the special role the media still occupy in public discourses and their role in forming public discourse, this relationship becomes the field that expresses with accuracy the degree of democracy, state accountability and, ultimately, citizenship in a society.

The involvement of the state in the media 'business' has been an intentional, strategic or unplanned course of action, and has taken various forms in the past. In addition, the degree and nature of involvement have not remained constant. As we saw in our discussion of the historical dimension of the British media, in Chapter 1, the state has intervened with laws and policies regarding prices, the material deemed publishable, labour relations and other areas. The state has therefore exercised control over a number of aspects of media activity, such as the economics of media, content-related questions and censorship, as well as defining the very structure of national media landscapes. When addressing this relationship, it is important to direct our focus towards the influence of policies that are designed to deal with these issues, as the area of law and policy is where the legitimization of certain ideas and codes of conduct takes place. The factors influential in policy-making and the most important policies currently effective are discussed later in this book. However, it is also important to consider other aspects of this relationship that are not always straightforward. Often, it is argued that the state attempts to manipulate the media or exercise control over their content. This is certainly one aspect and, as we have seen in the few examples at the start of this section, it has become increasingly necessary for governments to 'manage' media output that is related to the image of that government or its specific policies.

However, the media and communication companies, not only as transnational but also as national companies, need the state to function as provider and guarantor of stability within a specific national space. In the era of globalization, the spaces where these companies are active are also transnational. The barriers decline, trade tariffs decrease and the harmonization of laws is a function that states 'fulfil' in a system of global economy and international agreements. In this era, it is the case that companies, and in particular communication- and media-related ones, can hardly remain exclusively national if they want to carry on making a profit. Transnational companies can offer opportunities for further investment in a country, open up employment positions, even bring in technologies that can be disseminated in appropriate sectors. The economy of a country can benefit from the investment that comes from a transnational, even if this is in an area as sensitive as that of media. However, as Dicken (2003) also notes, this is the ideal scenario. As companies are, by definition, engineered to be competitive and exploitative, 'sharing' technology is not in their list of 'things to do'.

On the other hand, cultural and consumption changes also occur, and they are driven through the experience of working for a company or consuming its products. Sky One, as well as Sky's premium channels, for example, dedicate most of their airtime to US-produced series and programmes. A number of such programmes have also been 'copied' and translated into British productions, and today we can see many of these on British channels (Channel 4 or Five), such as traffic dramas, reality shows, hospital dramas or talk shows that are equivalent to *Oprah* or *Jerry Springer*, such as *Trisha* on ITV. The dependency that is being cultivated can, however, often turn the state into a mere facilitator of favourable environments for companies to expand into the national market. Certainly, the relationship between state and media is not one that can be described as one-way, as it is clear that the state uses the media for its own purposes too. Most notably, this is in terms of propaganda, whether this is in the guise of public information, such as a new policy that helps single parents, or part of a media campaign to influence public opinion. Such was the case of the 'Iraq dossier' and the Hutton Inquiry, where much doubt was expressed about the validity of government claims: it was argued that statements given as 'facts' had been tampered with to provide a more dramatic image of the situation and to persuade the British people (but also international audiences abroad and in the country, since this was a matter to be dealt with under the jurisdiction of the UN and therefore the international community) about the motive behind the attack on Iraq as one against a repressive regime. Dicken argues that the whole process of negotiation between transnationals and the state is a dynamic one. By the same token, 'negotiation' does not mean something that takes place on equal terms for both sides.

Digitization

Another important trend in contemporary British media is the process of digitization – that is, the conversion of analogue media, such as television and radio, to digital. This technology enables a larger number of channels to be transmitted (and therefore received and consumed) than analogue, not only on terrestrial television, but also, once in place, on cable and satellite. We have seen that the development of the British media landscape has already been affected by cable and satellite. Technology has played an important role in the liberalization of the telecommunications system, a necessary precondition for the liberalization of the broadcasting services.

Although discussions referring to the possibilities of digital technology took place as early as the late 1980s, it was in the mid-1990s that the British government included its dissemination as part of its media policy (Goodwin 1998: 149). Britain found itself leading the way to digital terrestrial television. The system works with the conventional antenna but requires a digital decoder box; digital cable and satellite function in a similar way. The debate about digital was wrapped in the colours of progress, a first taste of the 'information superhighway', something that would boost UK media and industry, etc. Some of the claims, such as the potential of interactive television to hook audiences into a more 'democratic' and exciting use of their TV sets, as well as high hopes for a bright rejuvenation of the British media industry did not quite materialize. As we have seen, 'foreign' ownership is the rule rather than the exception in British media, while interactive television – apart from the fact that democratization of communications requires a bit more than the interactive red button on the remote control – is only now starting to provide some possibilities for 'interaction' worthy of mention. Certainly the best interactive service by far is that provided by the BBC for its educational programmes (documentaries, mini-scientific and historical series, and other similar programmes) although it is also possible that games, quizzes and of course shopping (which is what free, non-subscription cable channels offer) is another pathway to interactivity.

Satellite-to-home digital TV was introduced by BSkyB and terrestrial digital was launched by the Granada/Carlton combined effort OnDigital. Finally, digital cable was launched by those cable companies that already dominated the cable market. Digital services have the capacity to broadcast hundreds of channels and pay-TV services, such as films-only or other events. BBC, Channels 4 and Five are broadcast through all these services, while the BBC has developed its own digital channels. It cannot easily be argued that the digital project has been a success. OnDigital (later relaunched as ITV Digital) died a slow and painful death: BSkyB already had the audiences and the money necessary to send OnDigital to oblivion. Technical problems with the service did not help either. BSkyB bought the exclusive sports rights to the UK soccer Premiership while ITV Digital was left with Nationwide football and fewer viewers. Through fierce competition, ITV Digital was forced out of the market.

BSkyB is a British-registered company, but it belongs to Australian Rupert Murdoch, as we have seen. Favourable treatment by both the Tory and New Labour governments has protected Murdoch's media (*The Times* and *The Sunday Times* earlier) from harsh laws. BSkyB was exempt from anti-concentration law when it merged with (and killed off) British Satellite Broadcasting in the late 1980s. Labelled 'non-domestic' (although British registered!) BSkyB dominated the market. This is a good example of the relationship between the state and major corporate powers. It also shows that the effects of policy are long term, with serious implications not simply in terms of economics, but also in terms of culture and politics. BSkyB rules the British market. Yet the public's interest in digital television is not particularly pronounced, partly because the complete switch-off from analogue to digital that the government has announced for 2010 entails high costs for consumers, who have to purchase new television sets or set-top boxes and perhaps new antennae. Its unpopularity is also due to the fact that the quality difference between analogue and digital pictures is minimal, the interactive services on offer are limited or extremely slow, and the programmes shown are re-runs of US productions or have already been broadcast on the free-to-air channels. ITV Digital's frequencies have been taken over by the BBC and BSkyB's partners (see also Curran and Seaton 2003).

Despite the enormous changes in the British media landscape in the last decade, and despite the fact that public service broadcasting was seriously undermined by government and private sector alike, the BBC has remained the main British 'institution' (see Chapter 7).

FURTHER READING

McChesney R. W. (2003) Corporate Media, Global Capitalism. In Cottle, S. (ed.), *Media Organization and Production*, London: Sage.
McChesney's political-economic approach to the study of media and communications is further expressed in this chapter, which describes the media systems in their inter-ownership patterns organized in tiers, according to the degree of corporate relations with each other. The core argument running through this chapter is that the processes of globalization require not only the intervention of the state but also extensive planning at an international level. This contradicts the claims of neo-liberalism that the market alone is the best organizer of social life.

Ross, K. (2001) Women at Work: Journalism as Engendered Practice, *Journalism Studies* 2(4): 531–44.

Ursell, G. (2000) Television Production: Issues of Exploitation, Commodification and Subjectivity in UK Television Labour Markets, *Media Culture and Society* 22: 805–25.
Though different in focus, both texts address the production and labour processes of the

British media today. Ross's text deals specifically with journalists and gendered experiences in the newsroom. Ursell's article discusses the changes brought into the production processes through commercialization and digitization. Both articles provide a good discussion of two seemingly different but closely interlinked dimensions of the world 'behind the scenes'.

Shahoul, J. (2001) Privatization: Claims, Outcomes and Explanations. In Philo, G. and D. Miller, *Market Killing: What the Free Market Does and What Social Scientists Can Do about it*, London: Longman.
A positioned piece about the shortcomings of the free market and the wave of privatization in Britain. A useful text that offers a critique and a comprehensive overview of the broader social and economic climate, and the context within which the contemporary media system is being shaped.

Walker, K. (2000) Public Service Broadcasting and New Distribution Technologies: Issues of Equality, Access and Choice in the Transactional Television Environment. In Wyatt, S., Henwood, F., Miller, N. and Senker, P. (eds), *Technology and In/equality: Questioning the Information Society*, London: Routledge.
The author argues that the new communication technologies of British television and in particular so-called interactive TV have not offered more choice to viewers and have not created a pluralistic media environment. The chapter discusses technological and policy developments in the field of television services in the UK during the 1990s.

chapter three

International aspects of media policy

European and global dimensions in British media policy

Globalization has not only affected the organization of media systems worldwide, it has also had an impact on the methods and directions of policy-making in the media and communications field. Until the 1980s, most European nation-states were, through their national governments, solely responsible for decisions regarding the operation of their media systems. In many ways, this meant that the state had significant control over the media and, in particular, the electronic media, television and radio. In Europe, the state generally enjoyed monopoly control over electronic media and was largely responsible for the direction of policy regarding national media. Since the mid-1980s, however, the actors involved, along with the direction and methods of media policy-making, have gradually changed. National media policy in Europe is now increasingly dependent on the direction of policy drawn up on a Europe-wide level, via the European Union (EU). Member states of the EU negotiate media regulation at a supranational level. Moreover, it is difficult to understand and analyse media policy in Europe without taking into account the changes that have taken place at an international level and their effects on global media policy. This chapter will look at the most significant media policy initiatives of the EU and seek to explain their influence over national policy. The discussion will expand to issues of global media and communication policy, with the aim of identifying those areas that are important to the cultural, social and political life and role of the British media.

The European Union – our new home?

The EU currently has 15 members, among which are some of the most economically powerful countries in the world (such as Germany and Great Britain). A number of other countries, most of them from the former Soviet bloc, have applied for membership of the EU. Britain has been a member of the EU (formerly the European Community, EC) since 1973, although this does not necessarily mean that, as a member, it has always been supportive of European integration. Even in the 1950s, long before the accession of Britain into the EC, and during the negotiations on the establishment of a European free trade area, which led to the Treaty of Rome in 1957, suspicions about European cooperation and an unwillingness to participate constructively have been two of the main characteristics of British involvement. This is partly due to 'cultural' reasons – the UK is an island, as opposed to the 'continent', and has a 'special relationship' with America – and partly to political reasons (Britain has, for instance, remained reluctant to engage in European integration). In the eyes of Europe, Britain does not play a fair game and is not committed to the European project. As a 'partner', the UK waits to see if specific measures taken in Europe become successful, and then decides whether it will follow them. This is often seen as an attempt to undermine the European project. For example, John Major, former UK Prime Minister, compared the EMU to a 'rain dance', causing great offence in other European countries (Middlemas, 1996: 723, n. 41). This has been the case with monetary integration in the form of the Economic and Monetary Union (EMU) in recent times (1992) and with the introduction of the euro in 2002: Britain is not yet participating. Still, the UK is a full EU member state and, as such, is involved in decision-making at a European level and obliged to comply with European regulation.

In very simple terms, EU regulation tends to have two main goals:

1. to harmonize national laws so that the internal European market can function
2. to make decisions on a more general legal framework and let details of the implementation of laws be arranged by nation-states.

Very often, criticisms of the EU refer to its lack of transparency in decision-making and the lack of accountability of some of its institutions (the European Commission, the European Parliament, the European Court of Justice and the Council of Ministers). Therefore, its legitimacy has often been questioned. The increasing power and role of the European Parliament in decision-making, however, tend to restore the balance and provide legitimacy to the EU. Despite these criticisms, which are often used by national governments for internal consumption, nation-states participate in decisions made within the EU context. They do this through their representatives in the Council of Ministers, while Members of the European Parliament represent nations and countries. Decisions made at a European level cannot be taken without the involvement and agreement of all member states. This means that Britain is also part of the current state of affairs of the EU.

Today, the EU is a highly complex and sophisticated system of governance, whose main objective is not simply economic integration; 375 million people live and work in the EU today, many of whom reside in places other than their country of origin. Transfers such as student and academic exchange programmes, holiday-makers, training programmes, franchises and company spin-offs contribute to internal human mobility at a pace that has turned spaces, and especially national capitals, into European metropolises. The EU has nine official working languages, but the Cirici Report estimated that the European area consists of 58 linguistic minorities (de Moragas Spa and Garitaonandia 1992: 224–5). European law becomes national law; British MEPs and administrators work together with Germans, Belgians, Greeks and Italians; European interests are represented in international agreements by the European Commission; the establishment of a European 'rapid reaction' military force and the increasing cooperation of security forces reinforce the impression that Europe is becoming a superstate.

Is Europe our new, extended family? This remains to be seen. A number of factors will be influential in the construction of a 'European' identity, if we accept that identity is a defining factor of people's self-perception. One of these factors is the degree of knowledge about our neighbouring societies, much of which has been poorly shaped by dominant stereotypes and presumptions about people and cultures. Moreover, personal experience of European cultures, and interpretation of this experience, may contribute to the creation of a new – additional – understanding of our place within Europe. Nevertheless, what seems to be important is the fact that the cultural sphere is among those where identities can be built. This is where the media are in a very strong position. This chapter will discuss some of the main European media policies and the way they affect media industries and their products.

Opening the market: television for all? The Television Without Frontiers Directive

One of the most important pieces of European legislation is the Television Without Frontiers (TVWF) Directive, for two reasons. First, this particular policy has been the most significant one in the promotion of the single market and, second, it is the first major policy directed at the media, a field where national states have had a relatively long and almost undisputed monopoly. The origins of this directive can be traced back to a report from the European Parliament (EP) in 1982 (European Parliament 1982). According to this report, conducted by Wilhelm Hahn, a German Christian Democrat MEP, television and radio were referred to as the 'chief media' in shaping public opinion and informing the citizens of Europe about the European Community. In order for the political elites to create links with the people whom they claimed to represent, the report called upon the Commission to initiate legislation that would protect media pluralism and encourage better communication links with Europeans through the launch of a proposed pan-European channel. (Only the Commission has the power to initiate formal legislation. At the time the European Parliament was significantly weak. Now the Commission and the Council of Ministers have to take into account the opinion of the European Parliament before they proceed. Moreover, the Council and the European Parliament are equal partners in decision-making. See, for example, Westlake (1994).) The EP was alarmed by the beginning of the commercialization of television and internationalization of American media, and what it saw as a danger to diversity of opinion and democracy. The EP was anxious for the EC to make policy that would take into account the political and social dimensions of new technologies, such as cable and satellite, and the new possibilities they offered.

The European Community, however, was built with mainly economic objectives in mind. The treaties did not allow the Commission to intervene in what were seen to be 'cultural' matters. As a legalistic solution, the Commission claimed that media products are services and that the process of media production belongs to the economic activities covered by the treaties. Free circulation of signals and services, along with freedom of mobility for workers and media companies and materials, were to be part of the Commission's jurisdiction. The harmonization of laws regarding broadcasting activities among European countries was, together with the circulation of content services, the main objective of the TVWF Directive. Almost a decade later, in 1989, and after a series of compromises between neo-liberalists and those who support a more protectionist approach, the directive became a reality.

The directive, the first of its kind in European territory and politics, laid the foundations for the single European market of cultural goods. Content and broadcasting would have no borders. The overarching aim of the directive was to harmonize national laws in such a way that would facilitate the liberalization of broadcasting activities within countries and encourage transborder trade of content, software, hardware and other resources. This was seen to be a necessary measure that would counter-balance Europe's 'deficiency' in programme trade vis-à-vis Japan (the champion of hardware) and the USA (the globally dominant content provider). The main disadvantage in European broadcasting production is considered to be the fact that Europe is a fragmented market. Unlike the US market, European markets have linguistic, cultural and geographical borders that make financial gains from the production and distribution of European works very uncertain. Differences in laws and regulation among countries only made Europe-wide production harder to achieve. Therefore, the directive was designed to tackle such problems. In 1997, it was amended, in order to 'update, clarify and complete' the 1989 provisions (Council Directive 97/36/EC). Some of the most important areas covered by the TVWF Directive are outlined below:

- Member states must ensure freedom of reception and retransmission of broadcasts from other member states within their own territory (Article 2a).

- Events of major importance to the public ('sports rights') must be broadcast without encryption, even if private broadcasters have bought exclusive rights. In particular, sports events such as the Olympic Games or the Football World Cup, but also other events that are considered to be of national or non-national importance, must be available 'entirely or partially' by live or deferred coverage. Each country is responsible for drawing up a list of such events (Article 3a).

- The directive provides a definition of European works (which was broadened by the 1997 amendment): European work is 'a production made under a bilateral co-production agreement between a Member State and a third country' (Article 6.4).

- The issue of content quota – whether European broadcasters should devote 50 per cent of their programming to works of European origin – has been a controversial issue since the discussion rounds preceding the 1989 directive. The majority of the European Parliament and some Commission Directorates have supported content quotas, in order to protect the European broadcasting industry. As in 1989 so in the 1997 text, content quotas were to be applied 'where practicable' (Article 6). This meant that broadcasters and member states were under no obligation to actively promote European works.

- According to Article 22, member states must take measures to ensure that programmes harmful to the development of minors are prohibited.

Although these are not the only provisions made by the directive, they are most characteristic of the objectives of this policy, which is more market-orientated than culture- or integration-centric. The immediate effect of the implementation of the directive was an enormous increase in the amount of programming of American products. Some of the strongest claims of the rationale behind the directive were to boost European production and distribution among European countries, and thereby create a European market. The creation of such a market would benefit the whole audiovisual sector in Europe, providing new job opportunities and strengthening the industry to compete with American programming. Instead of creating a European market for European products, however, the directive, partly due to its vague language, broadened the market for American imports. Commercial broadcasters were established in all European countries but they had little interest in promoting European works. Imports from the USA had increased ten-fold by 1992 (Vasconcelos in Collins 1999).

The UK has been in a more fortunate position than other European countries regarding broadcasting content. Content has always been exceedingly domestic, so the fact that neither broadcasters nor member states were required by the directive to promote European content through quotas, did not make a significant difference as far as terrestrial television and, in particular, public service broadcasters were concerned. One more important factor in this case is language: English is the dominant language of film and television exports, and Britain has benefited from its relationship with the American market, with exports to both the USA and Europe. However, British-based cable and satellite companies still depend heavily on American programming.

Public service broadcasting

Public service broadcasting, one of the few, and important, common European traditions, was criticized and undermined in the 1990s, not only by the public, as it is often seen to represent the interests of the state or the government, but also by private interests and neo-liberalist policies. Strong images associated with 'quality' and 'high culture' often go hand in hand with notions of bias or lack of objectivity. In the era of media liberalization, however, these criticisms aim to dismantle the public service character of broadcasters such as the BBC.

Public service broadcasters (PSBs) have different characteristics in different European countries, and have developed according to the specific socioeconomic and cultural conditions of each country. Multilinguistic countries, like Switzerland and Belgium, have developed PSBs that address such linguistic needs. Market size also plays an important role: German-language programmes produced by German PSBs are not only consumed within Germany but also by Austrian and Swiss audiences. Furthermore, market sizes have played an important role in defining methods of financing PSBs. Some have adopted the dual-financing system, which combines commercial advertising and licence fee, whereas others (such as the UK, Norway, Denmark and Sweden) rely totally on licence fees. The experience of the Second World War and the use of the media as tools of propaganda have also led European countries to guarantee freedom of expression in their constitutions. Furthermore, the experience of the era of deregulation and liberalization has also been different for PSBs. So, for example, the BBC has successfully managed to introduce new digital services, while its on-line presence, with news and features, was the most visited website in the UK in the first three months of 2001, with over 13 million visits and 320 million page impressions (ABC 2002). However, most PSBs have experienced a severe drop in their income and audiences with the introduction of private, commercial broadcasters. It is also interesting to note that the USA, Europe's big media rival, has a very weak, unsupported public broadcasting system (PBS) that, unlike major American conglomerates, plays only a marginal role in the American media market.

One of the most serious problems that European PSBs had to face, in terms of policy, was an attempt by the Commission, through the directorate for competition, to produce guidelines that would describe the role and rights of PSBs. These guidelines were the result of pressure exercised by private broadcasters, which claimed that subsidizing PSBs creates unfair competition conditions for commercial media. Furthermore, complaints about the expanding activity of PSBs, such as radio stations, on-line services and TV channels, pushed the direction of competition policy. At the same time, the PSBs themselves became concerned about losing their rights in the light of privatization.

The Commission produced guidelines that prescribed ways in which PSBs should be funded. To put it simply, PSBs and governments would have to make a decision as to how they finance their PSBs, whether this would be under:

- dual funding – a combination of state reimbursement and market competition
- unique funding – state funding being their only source of income
- public tenders – open to all operators seeking to produce public service programmes.

At the same time, member states should conform with a list of content that PSBs would not be allowed to broadcast, such as soap operas and other entertainment content (European Report). According to this argument, PSBs have a different role from commercial broadcasters. As such, they should fulfil their role (information and education) but not enter the areas that private broadcasters were covering (entertainment). The proposed guidelines had to be withdrawn as they invited strong reactions, both from the European Parliament, and the national governments and broadcasters. The European Parliament, working through the renowned Tongue Report (named after Labour MEP Carole Tongue) on public service broadcasting, defended the PSBs for their role in democratic societies, in the preservation of culture, addressing diverse interests and social groups, such as minorities, and their contribution in the production of European works. National governments, through their ministers, managed to come to an agreement and incorporate a protocol to the Treaty of Amsterdam which guarantees that it is the member state's responsibility to provide funding for the fulfilment of public service (European Communities 1997: paragraph 2).

Although this is a very important achievement, the Treaty of Amsterdam is the only international constitutional law in the world that guarantees the importance and survival of PSBs – the excessively liberalized media environment is hostile to European PSBs (Collins

1999). PSBs face serious problems in accessing programmes such as sports events where they have to compete on the open market for expensive programmes. Nevertheless, British terrestrial broadcasters are quite successful in comparison with other European PSBs.

The information society

The 'information society' is the European response to America's 'information superhighway' concept, declared by the Clinton–Gore administration in the late 1990s. Both concepts refer to the use of information as a source of wealth, capital, productivity and power in post-industrial societies (Van Dijk 1999). 'Information' is a broad term used to describe streams of data in banking, sciences or the military, for example, as well as news, reports and other already processed data distributed through and/or processed with the help of communication networks. The term 'information superhighway' refers to a future organization of communication networks that will have the technological capacity to integrate all current forms of data transmission and mass communication. To a certain extent this capacity is already partly available. However, the infrastructure necessary for this kind of technology is costly. The difference between industrially developed and developing countries is enormous. One typical example that illustrates this inequality is the fact that 88 per cent of the world's Internet users are concentrated in the northern hemisphere (Thussu 2000: 248). This is due not only to the high costs of installing telephone and cable lines, but also to inequalities in wages and access to education and training. The external debts of so-called 'third world' countries (mainly to Europe and the USA) are the main obstacle in the development of public services such as health-care provision, let alone investment in new technologies. In the western world today, however, we regard speedy communication as part of everyday life; this is especially the case for businesses and states in the most industrialized nations, where communication seems to transcend boundaries of time and space. Mobile phones, the Internet, computers that can be used as television sets, and television screens that can be used to access e-mails or shop on-line, on-line versions of the traditional press, or entirely on-line magazines and stores (media convergence), even the possibility of electronic voting and political participation are available to European, American, Australian and some Asian citizens.

The centrality of information in this new social order has given rise to the discussion of a number of issues. In particular, the need for additional or new legislation that can deal with these new realities and demands has become the subject of European as well as global policy (as will be discussed later in this chapter). The most important policy areas to have attracted the attention of the EU are users' privacy and data protection, and ownership and freedom of information. For the EU, even the development of the European audiovisual industry is examined in the light of the 'information revolution'. The 'information society' is seen to be the main driving force behind the technological advancement and expansion of already contested markets (Commission 1994). A key industry in the implementation of the ideas of the information society is telecommunications. Since 1 January 1996 all cable television networks have been permitted to provide all telecommunication services, and implementation for voice telephony opened up in 1998. The UK has been quickest to liberalize its telecommunications (Collins 1999: 159). Like the TVWF Directive, the principles emphasized by directives such as the Open Network Provision Directive (European Commission 1990a), Services Directive (European Commission 1990b) and Cable Directive (European Commission 1995) were the harmonization of national laws and the liberalization of services, while a common goal has been to disband monopolies. It was argued that privatization and liberalization promoted flexibility, and technological innovation therefore adapted new technologies faster and at a wider spectrum than under state/governmental or publicly owned monopolies. Yet, the impact of liberalization has not been according to prognoses. Rural areas in the UK could be forced to wait up to 20 years before they are offered high-speed Internet services, unless the UK government makes a significant financial contribution (Cyber-Society – Live, 6 February 2002). This means that no private company is willing to invest in rural and remote areas with few potential customers, which creates a number of problems, such as inaccessibility to technology for rural areas, and contributes further to inequalities in information access.

Privacy and the protection of personal data

The EU directive on the 'Protection of Individuals with Regard to the Processing of Personal Data and the Free Movement of Such Data' (Commission 1995) is, according to Van Dijk (1999: 136), 'the most stringent in the world'. It combines economic motives with some defence of human and civil rights. Like all other directives in the field of media and communications, the overarching – economic – principle has been to guarantee the 'free movement' of personal data under specified conditions. Here, personal data are recognized as factors of economic activity, given, however, the sensitive nature of privacy and the protection of individuals in democratic systems, the directive draws on human rights and civil liberties. It allows the collection of data only for specific and legitimate purposes. Data should be up to date and the 'data subjects' need to give their consent and have to be informed about the use of such data. Furthermore, the controllers (the agency or body that determines the purposes and uses of such data) are to be held responsible for their processing activities. An important provision of this directive is the definition of data that are not allowed to be processed at all, such as those that deal with political beliefs, race/ethnicity, data concerning health or sex life, and religious and philosophical beliefs.

The USA also has a number of laws governing personal data processing, but these impose no obligations on controllers. Moreover, data such as those on medical history are not protected from disclosure by law. Most attempts to improve the legal framework fail because of the enormous pressure brought to bear by businesses, such as marketing companies and federal intelligence (Miller in Van Dijk 1999: 136). As the European directive is valid only for members of the EU, there is no protection of personal data once disclosed to US-based controllers. More recently, after the events of 11 September 2001, the US government has been putting pressure on the EU to relax legislation in the protection of personal data, with the justification that a change in the law would allow more effective action against terrorism.

Whatever the motives, whether for (foreign or domestic) governments to have direct access to personal data or for American marketing and media companies to gain access to such data, or both, the outcome will be a severe blow to civil liberties around the world, as under the pretext of national or other security, individuals (especially those whose political or philosophical beliefs are considered a 'problem' by the state) will be left without adequate protection against private companies and state abuse alike. A sign of the likely potential violation of civil liberties is the proposal that the EU create databanks of 'suspected protestors', which will be held by the Schengen Information System on a centralized database (Statewatch 2001). At the time of writing, the European Parliament had approved measures giving member states the power to force telephone and Internet companies to retain the detailed communications logs of each of their customers for an unspecified period (Millar 2002). The British government has already given these rights to the police and intelligence forces, Customs & Excise and Inland Revenue. A bill to be debated in Parliament provides for the extension of data and communication surveillance by all public services, such as councils, the National Health Service, even the Departments of Transport and Health, among others. Surveillance, according to the proposed bill, will be extended to include the use of mobile phones, telephones, e-mails, websites and Internet activity. The government (and any government department) could then know the exact location of individuals at any given point in time, the exact e-mail correspondence (date, time, receivers, content) and activity on the Internet, such as websites visited.

Global policy issues

Since the Second World War, media and communication policies have increasingly become the object of an international, although not always equitable, global dialogue among governments, capital and civil society, comprised of non-governmental and other organizations and social movements (see Galtung 1999). As Galtung (1999: 9) notes, direct communication between state and civil society is known as 'democracy' and denotes the relationship between the two. According to Galtung, there are three bilateral relationships: state–capital, state–civil society and capital–civil society. Of these three relationships, only one is, he says, '(a) transparent to all, (b) institutionalised, (c) two-way and dialogical, (d) used for decisions binding on both parties and (e) broad or open to any topic' (1999: 9).

This is the relationship between state and civil society. It would be more realistic to argue that this relationship could and should be a relationship of equal dialogue and mutual respect. States exercise power, often at the expense of human rights. Internationally, governments have formed intergovernmental organizations (IGOs) such as the United Nations General Assembly, and capital is organized into transnational corporations (TNCs) and the International Chamber of Commerce and the World Economic Forum. As we have already seen, the number of transnational media corporations has grown enormously in the last 20 years and such organizations have pushed for changes in the regulatory framework of national and international (e.g. European) media. The quest for the creation of new markets through the expansion of technologically advanced media, whether hardware (technical infrastructure) or software (programmes and content), has put pressure on national governments to liberalize the communications sector. TNCs look for new sources of raw materials, new consumer markets, investment opportunities, low tax economies, low wages and low governmental control. The expansion of markets and the activities of TNCs do not, however, undergo a process of dialogue between capital and civil society. Citizens do not become involved in the decisions of media or other transnational companies, even though they are targeted by the TNCs' marketing departments and advertising. The products of media companies, such as news, soap operas and documentaries are also, to a great extent, responsible for this 'lack of dialogue' (Galtung 1999) as they tend to produce and reproduce stereotypes about nations, women, homosexuals and other social groups, and therefore reinforce specific 'dualisms' and 'binary oppositions'. These dualisms deprive people from having their voices heard, both in the production process of media messages and in their representation within media and cultural messages. Rush (1999) also argues that even the way human beings think, in 'dualistic, competitive, either-or' structures, is the consequence of a mechanistic, industrial model of production with profit-making its only objective. Inequitable distribution of resources, such as information, means that some parts of the world are excluded from the communication process, since they have little or no access to communication infrastructures (such as computers) or are excluded from the process of producing their own meanings. So, for example, the so-called 'third world' has very limited means to produce its own meanings and represent itself, due to the unequal distribution of resources. Thus, those who do possess the means of production of meanings, equipment and distribution systems, tend to represent their own views about the developing world. These images and meanings, filtered and distorted, are also distributed back to the developing countries. The colonial relationship of information flow and communication between north and south produces and reproduces structural inequalities and dangerous misrepresentations (Masmoudi 1979: 172–3, quoted in Thussu 2000: 44). In similar ways (distorted) communication relations disadvantage women and other social groups, thereby re/producing them as the 'Other', outside the norm, standard universal being. The 'norm', according to Rush (1999: 71) and other feminist researchers, is white, heterosexual men, who own the media, national or international, and therefore have the power to produce meanings that silence and misrepresent already disadvantaged groups.

The MacBride Report

In 1978, the UNESCO General Conference recognized in its Mass Media Declaration the role of mass media in the development of 'third world' countries, and later that year the United Nations General Assembly adopted a resolution on the New World Information and Communication Order (NWICO). One year later, the International Commission for the Study of Communication Problems (MacBride Commission), via its report to UNESCO, turned media and communication issues into matters of global significance. The MacBride Commission consisted of 15 scholars from five continents and studied the role of the media in information flow, and the ways that the media could become educators about world problems.

Among the recommendations of the commission, those that referred to the democratization of communication were the most controversial. The report stated that the problems of imbalance of information, illiteracy and semi-literacy, lack of technology and the exclusion of disadvantaged groups seriously undermined the democratization of communication systems. The ways to overcome these obstacles, according to the commission, related to the structural reconfiguration of media systems that would include (a) the participation of civil society in the management of media organizations; (b) horizontal information – as opposed to the top-to-bottom existing form of communication practice; and (c) three forms of alternative communication: radical opposition, community or local media movements and trade unions or other social groups (Thussu 2000: 46). Western countries undermined the proposals for a New World Information and Communication Order. In particular the USA, strongly supported by the UK, termed the NWICO the voice of communist propaganda. Both countries, two of the strongest UNESCO members, withdrew from the organization in the early 1980s, giving a 'warning' in an attempt to halt all studies related to the NWICO throughout the decade (Nordenstreng 1999). In the 1990s, the discourses of NWICO were still alive, although perhaps under different names and with a different rhetoric. Seriously threatened by the US and UK governments, and the neo-liberalist ideologies that swept global politics and policies in the 1990s, the recommendations and the issues addressed by the MacBride Report continued to surface on global agendas – this time, those of academics, non-governmental organizations (NGOs) and organizations of the civil society in general. The MacBride roundtable continued its work until the end of 1990s when it joined the Communication Rights Platform.

Freedom of expression

Article 19 of the Universal Declaration of Human Rights, adopted by the United Nations General Assembly in 1948, states that:

> Everyone has the right to freedom of opinion and expression; this right includes freedom to hold opinions without interference and to seek, receive and impart information and ideas through any medium and regardless of frontiers.

Also, according to Article 10 of the European Convention for the Protection of Human Rights and Fundamental Freedoms:

> Everyone has the right to freedom of expression. This right shall include freedom to hold opinions and to receive and impart information and ideas without interference by public authority and regardless of frontiers. This article shall not prevent States from requiring the licensing of broadcasting, television or cinema enterprises.
>
> (Council of Europe 1950/1998)

Examining these articles closely, two general dimensions of the right to freedom of expression can be discerned: the right to express an opinion/idea or information, and the right to receive the same. The right to receive information presupposes the right to seek (i.e. actively search for) information. Furthermore, the rights to 'freedom of expression' and 'freedom of information' must be protected by the state according to international law, even if these rights have to be protected against the state itself. The right to freedom of expression and information has mainly been designed with a hierarchical top-down communication structure in mind. It was intended to protect human rights with reference to state violations and abuses of power. As such, it does not protect the right to freedom of expression against other powerful non-state groups such as economic or other forces that can be seriously restrictive. Hamelink (1995: 303) points to the possibility of concentration of power in the hands of individuals, but also the power of citizens to restrict the freedom of expression of fellow citizens. One such example can be argued to be the power of media conglomerates to filter information sent and received, as well as to 'allow' or promote the expression of certain actors or values and not others. Freedom of expression 'without interference' refers to interference by public authority. The right does not provide protection from interference by other forces, such as economic forces.

Freedom of information mainly refers to the right of the citizens to seek, receive and impart information. Preconditions for exercising this right are access to information held or administered by public or private sources, the right to not be misinformed (deceived) and the right to access means for the distribution of information. These rights imply an open and democratic system where information channels are available to citizens, to access and convey information. The role of the media here is to seek and receive information on public matters. In doing so, the media have the moral responsibility not merely to broadcast messages provided by (powerful) sources such as the state, but also to make sure that the information received is correct and true. The ultimate goal is for the media to be in a position to scrutinize the government. Hence, press freedoms such as the protection of sources must also be guaranteed.

Furthermore, the media and citizens have the right to impart information. The special significance of the role of the media in imparting information in a truthful way also implies that the public should have access to them. The latter is a particularly fragile issue as the structures and operations of the press prohibit involvement of the public (at least the direct involvement). In numerous cases, the European Court of Human Rights has provided very clear rulings about the role of journalists and the media in the protection of the right to freedom of expression.

> Protection of journalistic sources is one of the basic conditions for press freedom, as is reflected in the laws and the professional codes of conduct in a number of Contracting States and is affirmed in several international instruments on journalistic freedoms .... Without such protection, sources may be deterred from assisting the press in informing the public on matters of public interest. As a result the vital public-watchdog role of the press may be undermined and the ability of the press to provide accurate and reliable information may be adversely affected. Having regard to the importance of the protection of journalistic sources for press freedom in a democratic society and the potentially chilling effect an order of source disclosure has on the exercise of that freedom, such a measure cannot be compatible with Article 10 (art. 10) of the Convention unless it is justified by an overriding requirement in the public interest.
>
> (European Court of Human Rights 1996: Goodwin vs UK)

And:

> . . . the dominant position which the Government occupies makes it necessary for
> it to display restraint in resorting to criminal proceedings, particularly where
> other means are available for replying to the unjustified attacks and criticisms of
> its adversaries or the media. . . . the pre-eminent role of the press in a State
> governed by the rule of law must not be forgotten. Although it must not overstep
> various bounds set, inter alia, for the prevention of disorder and the protection of
> the reputation of others, it is nevertheless incumbent on it to impart information
> and ideas on political questions and on other matters of public interest.
>
> (European Court of Human Rights 1992: Castells vs Spain)

Both extracts show that the right to freedom of expression and of information was intended
to refer predominantly to relations with the state. Civil organizations and academics have
pointed out the delimitations of the right and called for a normative regulatory framework
that provides for the protection of the right against structural, institutional and other
restrictions. This is called the right to communicate and refers to the comprehensive nature of
human and mass communication, which is a broader definition of the right to freedom of
information and was developed by Jean D'Arcy in 1979. D'Arcy was concerned about the
development of a society in which the division between media and message producers and
those who can only consume them is deepening (Kleinwaechter 1999). The concept of the
right to communicate implies a moral responsibility towards the *social process* of
communicating on behalf of the 'information-rich' countries, states, public authorities or
private groups and people to actively enable free communication among free people, even by
sharing resources with the 'information-poor' (Hamelink 1995: 294). Several UNESCO
study groups and debates since 1980 have failed to arrive at a satisfactory definition of the
right to communicate as a human right. Critics have pointed out that the 'right' takes on a
regulatory dimension and, as such, communication will have to be legislatively and
conceptually interpreted. The problem is that interpretation will be made by those groups
already in power and not those the right aims to protect (Hamelink 1995).

Freedom of information

Although the UK is obliged to respect the right to freedom of expression and freedom of
information, it has not managed to incorporate this in its legislative structure for nearly 20
years. The Freedom of Information (FOI) Act 2000 was finally approved in November 2000.
By 2005, the government must have implemented the act but it has yet to start. According to
the act, the general right of access to information is guaranteed. However the exceptions to
the right are so numerous that the government has been criticized by NGOs (e.g. Amnesty
International) and politicians for designing law on the protection of freedom of information
that is effectively more restrictive than the current code of conduct.

The act is restrictive when information related to a number of areas – policy formulations,
ministerial communications, investigations and proceedings, 'the effective conduct of public
affairs', factual information and its analysis, research findings, scientific assessments, evidence

of health hazards, reports on overseas practice, cost data, technical assumptions and consultants' studies – is concerned. Furthermore, information that can be released is limited to areas where decisions have already been made, and sensitive areas such as defence, international relations, economy, crime prevention and immigration, along with police and the intelligence agencies, are excluded.

One important safeguard is the clause on the 'public interest test'. Under the act, any withholding of information must be to serve the public interest. The public interest test in the new UK act and in the pending Bosnian bill requires that information or materials otherwise found to be exempt may be released if 'public benefit in knowing the information outweighs any harm that may be caused from disclosure' (Banisar 2001). This is a condition that the British legislators had to take into account, since the act could be found to be in conflict with the European Convention on Human Rights (ECHR) and its rulings. Law may, according to Article 34 of the Constitution, restrict the exercise of the freedom of information. The term 'law' applies to statutes adopted by Parliament. The statute 'On Information' does not, however, cover 'confidential information possessed by [the] state'. The Information Commissioner will oversee both the Freedom of Information Act and the Data Protection Act 1998. The national Hungarian, Canadian and German provincial models illustrate a new trend of placing the national data protection authority in charge of overseeing freedom of information too. The new UK and Estonian laws also include this provision (Banisar 2001). However, in the UK, the minister of the department concerned can in some cases overrule the Commissioner's decision.

Currently, there are several restrictions on freedom of information in UK law. The Official Secrets Act (OSA) 1989 was used recently against journalist Tony Geraghty in response to his book *The Irish War*, which details surveillance techniques used in Northern Ireland and the UK by the police and intelligence services. Another journalist was arrested under the OSA in February 2000 for communicating with former intelligence agent David Shayler (see e.g. Article 19 1999).

However, access to governmental information sources is not the only dimension of the right to freedom of information. As discussed above, the right also implies that citizens have the right to truthful and accurate information, whether from private or public authority sources. Violations of human rights do not only take place in 'far away' countries or under repressive regimes. Human rights are very fragile in that those in power can easily violate them. This does not mean that the violation of human rights is acceptable; it demonstrates, however, that civil society has to be alert to such violations and actively oppose them. Although it is true that violations of the human right to freedom of information are closely related to the relationship of the media with society, they also extend to all areas of human and social life.

The Irish Parliament approved a draft Abortion Information Bill two and a half years after public referenda voted in favour of the right to travel and freedom of expression to be preserved despite prohibition of abortion in Ireland. These proposals would bring Irish law into compliance with international law and ECHR decisions. The bill guaranteed the freedom to provide information about legal abortion in other countries – abortion in Ireland being prohibited even in the case of pregnancy resulting from rape. However, the bill also restricted the right by decreeing that information should be given only to people who *request* it. This is problematic because it limits clinics' and doctors' ability to notify the general public about abortion services available abroad. It also prevents people from requesting the service because they do not know *how* to request the information. Such information should be provided without any advocacy on abortion (Human Rights Watch Women's Rights Project 1995: 448–51). These conditions restrict the right to freely impart information regardless of frontiers. They also restrict the right of freedom of expression in order to protect certain 'morals' over others that are not shared by all people. In addition, they are likely to cause difficulties in the doctor–patient relationship, as doctors would not be free to advise a woman to terminate her pregnancy if her life was in danger.

Conclusions

The processes of globalization have influenced the ways in which media and communications policy is made, and this is not confined to national boundaries. On the contrary, policy is made at various levels – national, regional and international – and it is clear that, to a great extent, there are media policy issues and problems that cut across nations. Two such issues are the universal human right to freedom of expression and the right to freedom of information. Despite the fact that such rights have been included in the most fundamental universal legal charter – that of the human rights – this does not mean that they exist unchallenged by governments, even in democratic western countries.

FURTHER READING

Jäckel, A. (2003) *European Film Industries*, London: bfi: Chapter 4.
A comprehensive chapter discussing in great detail production strategies and policies in Europe. Major policy initiatives are referred to as is their impact on European production, within which the reader can place the UK position in a comparative setting.

McPherson, C. (2000) Death to the Entrepreneur: An Examination of the Use of Technology and Legislation to Control Programme Piracy at the Dawn of the Digital Era. In Lees, T., Ralph, S. and Langham Brown, J. (eds), *Is Regulation Still an Option in a Digital Universe?* Luton: University of Luton Press.
The chapter examines practices of piracy in relation to digital satellite television and, in particular, access to programmes. It discusses the policy initiatives taken and considered by the EU in that respect and makes reference to the entrepreneurial losses suffered.

Reading, A. (1999) Campaigns to Change the Media. In Stokes, J. and Reading, A. (eds), *Media in Britain: Debates and Developments*, London: Macmillan.
This chapter offers a comprehensive discussion of the ideological and cultural underpinnings of cultural and media policy, and the organized attempts of the public to change the media. The author divides such attempts into three categories: those that relate to media morality, those with the aim of achieving greater participation on the part of the public, and those that address discriminatory media practices against certain groups of people.

chapter four

Media policy in Britain

The previous chapter explored some of the most important media policy issues in the world today. As we have seen, international institutions increasingly take the decisions that determine the development and role of the media in contemporary societies. Part of the reason for this is the fact that, in this era of intense globalization, the issues surrounding media and communications become of common concern across nations and cultures. Another reason for the internationalization of policy-making is that the media, especially the transnational media companies, operate in a host of countries and national markets. This means that their activity becomes difficult to regulate, control or manage within the limited capacities of a nation-state. Capital, goods and services in the audiovisual sector, Internet-based business and content, radio programmes and films, video games and computer software are all subject to transborder trade and are consumed by millions of people around the globe. The task of managing such huge economic operations, but also dealing with their possible effects on local cultures and nation-states, requires international coordination of trade activities and technical standards.

At the same time, the undeniable significance of the media and communication processes in human societies places these 'industries' in a quite distinct position. The press is not seen simply in terms of its ability to attract advertising or reach large audiences. The role of the press in forming public opinion and informing the public is regarded as a very important one. That is why constitutional laws in many countries protect this role. The objectives of freedom of expression and access to information bring together two major actors in media policy: the state and the market. As discussed earlier, in an international context, the state and the market affect content and the ways that it is organized. The amount of text in newspapers, and also the approach to some issues reported in the press, are influenced by the relationships between the press and advertisers. The freedom to seek state-held information, the decisions relating to visual texts of sexually explicit material, the freedom to express dissent through the means of demonstration or virtual protest, or even the right to send e-mails and create Internet content are, similarly, subject to a degree of state control.

This chapter takes a closer look at the British experience. It will focus on the media policy that led to the Communications Bill 2002 and will aim to show the ways in which national policy is not only influenced by, but also has an impact on, international processes.

Structural issues

The Broadcasting Act 1990

The Broadcasting Act signalled a forceful competitive broadcasting environment in the British media landscape. It is a major piece of policy that, in many ways, crystallized the repeated attempts of UK Conservative governments to commercialize the broadcasting space. As discussed in Chapter 1, the Peacock Committee – a committee assigned by Margaret Thatcher to look into the future of broadcasting and in particular the role of the public service broadcasting – recommended the opening up of the market to private broadcasters and funding through advertising for Channel 4. The government expected (indeed, had been hoping for) a negative report about the BBC, which would provide the rhetorical and discursive justification to alter the form of funding or even the character of the institution. Despite the fact that the Peacock Committee was selected because of its negative predisposal toward public service broadcasters, it did not make the recommendations Thatcher had hoped for. Instead, the Peacock Committee defended the quality and status of the BBC and dismissed the possibility of replacing the licence fee with advertising funding on grounds of possible deterioration of content quality. The Broadcasting Act 1990 draws some of its material directly from the Peacock Report recommendations of 1986, but it also ignores some of the most positive recommendations for the long-term future of the BBC (Goodwin 1999: 137).

The Broadcasting Act 1990 established two new regulatory bodies: the Independent Television Commission (ITC) and the Radio Authority (which replaced the IBA and the Cable Authority respectively). The role of the ITC was to regulate and control the licensing of all commercial television services. Now, licensing new television services entailed the duty of these services to follow certain rules and fulfil obligations. In the case of non-compliance, service providers could even be penalized with the withdrawal of their licence. These conditions, alongside that of 'quality threshold', were introduced to demonstrate that accountability and the free market are not two contradictory conditions. The new channels were required to dedicate sufficient time to high-quality news and current affairs programmes, and provide programming for children. The new status quo required that licences would be given to the highest bidder, introducing in this way the characteristics of the free market, realized through a supply–demand relationship.

Furthermore, the ITC had to ensure the competitiveness of this new market by determining 'fair' competition and distribution (or provision) of services across the UK. In other words, the rhetoric of universality and quality was used in reference to principles that were deeply entrenched in the *raison d'être* of the public service broadcasting system, the system the country was most familiar with. Of course one should not confuse rhetoric with reality. The reality of the expansion of services throughout the UK was predominantly to do with the creation of markets, and the commercialization of broadcasting and cultural products. The opening up of more spaces for markets was one reason why, under the new system, Channel 4 was to be partly financed by advertising.

The act also demonstrated the implications of technological convergence in the policy environment. Convergence – the multiplicity of function of communication media – becomes more apparent with the participation of telecommunications companies in offering conduits for cable TV. This act, which amended the Telecommunications Act 1984, regulated the sending of offensive or indecent messages via a public telecommunications system and therefore via cable television. Furthermore, the Obscene Publications Act 1959/1964 was also now included within the scope of the new policy. This meant that content, whether carried via satellite, terrestrial or cable on to our screens, was regulated in terms of 'taste' and 'decency'. Although the Tory government pursued a neo-liberal, market-orientated policy trajectory as far as media ownership was concerned, it maintained a paternalistic and elitist approach to content. The Broadcasting Standards Council, established in 1988 and given statutory powers under the 1990 act, became the content 'watchdog' in matters of violence and sex. This might be perceived to be at odds with the neo-liberal argument that individuals know best where their interests lie and should therefore remain free to pursue such interests. The argument is meant to emphasize the 'necessity' of deregulated and therefore 'free' markets. It is very possible, as Goodwin also notes (1999) that pro-market governments remain deeply conservative in matters of content. The Broadcasting Act brought a paternalistic philosophy of cultural products to the area of British policy. It may be of interest to note that laws regarding 'decency' and 'taste' constitute a very *British* policy feature, as such laws (censorship on the grounds of 'taste' and 'decency') either do not exist or are very modest in the rest of Europe.

Another point worthy of note is the role of EU in UK media policy. As discussed in the previous chapter, the UK is an integral part of the decision-making process at EU level. As a member of the polity, the UK has to abide by the laws it also helps to create. The Television Without Frontiers (TVWF) Directive – the European law that creates a single European media market by ensuring the free circulation of goods and services, such as media products and broadcasting services across the countries of Europe – is one such example. The act reflected on the requirements of the Directive and implemented them. One of the requirements was that member states should allow the free circulation of goods and services, such as the transmission of programmes. In some cases, this would mean that adult television channels could be broadcast in UK territory with programmes that would not necessarily be acceptable to British law, particularly in terms of the Obscene Publications Act. Such channels are subscription-based and their content abides by special restrictions as defined by British law.

The directive, although all-embracing in its geographic authority, remains vague enough for national laws to be able to adjust it according to specific cultural and other traditions. Furthermore, one very important provision of the directive, that of content quotas for European works, is also embraced by the act. Although the BBC had always shown predominantly national programmes, the situation changed with the introduction of commercial channels in the UK. An immediate concern, expressed not only in the Peacock Report but also by academics and MPs critical of deregulation, was regarding the dominance of US products in the newly commercialized media landscape. Such programmes have become especially attractive to broadcasters because they offer quantity (many programme hours) at a low cost. The dominance of soap operas, series and films produced in the USA is a problem faced by every country in Europe.

ITV licensees are required to reserve 25 per cent of their total output for independent producers. The philosophy behind this clause is the belief that national and European works need the protection of law. In other words, if the state does not force broadcasters to 'make room' for independent (and home-made productions), the European content industry will not be able to compete with powerful Hollywood. Another requirement, in the spirit of EU legislation eager to demonstrate its interest in linguistic and other minorities, was to affirm measures for the promotion of such minorities. The Gaelic Television Committee was set up to fulfil this provision and oversee the production of television programmes in Gaelic. The act, however, also demonstrates that although the motives behind the liberalization of audiovisual services in Britain were largely market-driven, the sentiments behind specific parts of the policy remained fixed on ideas of quality, national product and moral control over content. These characteristics may not hold the same weight for all aspects of the broadcasting industry and services, but they remained important even throughout the most aggressive period of liberalization of media.

The Broadcasting Act 1996: the road to cross-ownership

The Broadcasting Act 1996 went a step further in the liberalization of the media market and introduced allowances for the emergence of cross-ownership. National newspaper owners with less than 20 per cent market share in the press market were allowed ownership of private broadcasting companies and control of non-domestic satellite broadcasters. Rupert Murdoch's dominance of 30 per cent of the newspaper market, as well as BSkyB (FT 20 November 2001) was a target of the new policy. These allowances 'fluctuate' according to the already accumulated circulation (the lower the circulation, the higher the number of radio licences). However, even newspaper owners who control more than 50 per cent of the circulation are allowed to own one licence. This measure is 'subject to public interest test' but 'public interest' can become a very vague and unhelpful concept that has little practical application (depending on who has the authority to define it). Interestingly, in cases where the 'extent' of public interest requires clarification, it is not the public whose judgement will be sought.

Similar policy decisions were adopted for terrestrial broadcasters and regional media. In response to the argument over concentration, it is reasonable to assume that the measures introduced to limit audience share of broadcasters to 15 per cent provide some restrictions to the domination of the market. As we will discuss later in this chapter, further measures were proposed in the Communications Bill 2002 that sought to remove more restrictions and limits to ownership concentration.

The problem of concentration of ownership has been dealt with by various policies in different European countries. Germany applies restrictions on the numbers of companies (channels) owned by any one corporation. Greece has always encouraged cross-ownership, based on the idea that media companies have enough experience and knowledge of the Greek media market to have good prospects. The USA is leaning strongly towards lifting ownership and audience restrictions, as policies are claimed to have become 'obsolete' in a market dominated by satellite and cable technology that allows a large number of broadcasters to enter. The EU has not managed to make policy on the matter of ownership concentration and pluralism despite repeated calls from the European Parliament, which demonstrates not only the difficulty but also the pressures and the commercial interests that are at stake if restrictive policy is imposed. The main argument in favour of deregulation of ownership restrictions is one that emphasizes the logic of the market benefiting from economic activity of that particular level. However, the ITV channels maintained their complicated ownership structure and organization, based on the operation of regional channel divisions and their subsequent 'fragmentation' into the ownership of 18 companies, also owned by a complex system of investors. Some form of cross-ownership can be found here – mainly, however, in terms of cross-holdings.

The concentration of ownership in the hands of a few media organizations is supported by measures that encourage powerful companies to invest in other forms of media. For example, press owners can acquire radio and television stations. The immediate problem resulting from cross-ownership in a country or region is the fact that the very argument *for* the liberalization of the market – that is, the entry of more media sources and therefore products – is undermined. The diversity of sources shrinks rather than expands. As Aidan White, General Secretary of the International Association of Journalists, comments in *OpenDemocracy* (2002), 'Media conglomerates exercise enormous influence as they jostle for leadership in the global media economy, competing furiously for access to mass markets in Asia, Europe and Latin America. But they don't only make money. They make politics, too.' Such pressures, as well as relationships of dependence cultivated with politicians, shape the conditions of an environment unfavourable to questions of quality, independence, investigation and critique. When the market imperative becomes the least common denominator of policy (whether this is regulation designed by the state or organizational policy devised by the media corporations for their own strategic planning), standards of quality are the first victim. This means that under the logic of rationalization that involves cutting down costs and maximizing profits, strategies are employed that make market – and not, for example, quality – sense. Principles largely agreed to be vital for the minimum operation of democratic systems, such as critique or diversity of information, can easily be ignored if they prove to be unprofitable.

The Broadcasting Act 1996 complies with EU regulation on major events (such as the Olympic Games or the Eurovision Song Contest), which requires member states to provide lists of these, and for which private broadcasters will not be able to acquire exclusive rights. The act introduced a code for the acquisition of rights to listed events. The public service broadcasting system, having remained at the centre of controversial debates about its place, role and character in modern British society, managed to retain its main funding source: the licence fee. Proposals to reorganize the BBC into separate independent companies – a strategy that would potentially be harmful to the financial viability of BBC, and also its capability to produce quality programming – echoing similar plans from the Thatcher era, were abandoned. But only for the time being. The BBC was finally granted permission to expand commercially, while the licence fee (with an extension until 2006) continued to be the funding source of the PSB.

Regulating content

So far we have discussed the extent and ways in which British national policy has sought to inform media structures. As we have seen, although media policy is predominantly an exercise largely determined by the government, it is not independent of international media policy developments or of the changing communication structures and the market. These relations of interdependence are reflected in the national media system of a country. For example, Britain, due to its membership of the EU, has to take into account minimum legislative requirements as defined by EU law. Similarly, commercialization of the mass media worldwide, directly or indirectly, has had an impact on public service broadcasters. The British PSB system is also experiencing the effects of this.

Media policy also depends on the ideological convictions of a government, the power of interest groups and private media corporations to lobby effectively for a certain policy, the conditions created by previous policy, as well as the degree to which the public has a role in the process. The major changes that have taken place in the media landscape in the last 20 years have concentrated on the structural arrangement of the media. This arrangement involves media ownership, the use of the broadcasting spectrum and size of audiences reached, as well as changes to the production and dissemination of programmes due to technological developments. It would be a mistake, however, to assume that policy directed at structural aspects of the media has no effect on the nature of media content. As we have seen, the importance of the question of 'who owns the media' lies precisely in the issue of control over content. And control over content means control over public opinion, and power to influence the politics of a society. Goodwin (1999) argues that although the intentions of successive Tory governments have been to liberalize the media sector in its financial economic sense, it has not been their intention to create the conditions for freer media in terms of content. However, similarly, little can be said in defence of 'New Labour'.

Content and war

The importance of media content is evident in the repeated (more often than not successful) attempts of governments to control information and the tone (perspective) of reporting during wars. Military and governmental control over access to primary and alternative sources, as well as over reports, is a serious concern for all societies that claim to be democratic. Recent practices have seriously compromised material made available through war reporting, leaving audiences with 'war correspondence' that provides a lot of information, but with little substance. Such examples are the detailed reports on the numbers, type and generation of weapons used by the NATO during the Gulf, Kosovo and Afghanistan wars. Such reports usually concentrate on the technological supremacy of the military – information that is heavily dependent on press releases issues by the spokes*men* (usually) of the Ministries of Defence and Foreign Affairs, and the military establishment. Due to the lack of investigative journalism and/or self-censorship of journalists, information about the destructiveness and long-term effects of weapons, as well as side-effects for those using them (not to mention the stark reality of their fatal effects), becomes available, if at all, only after the event and only when it is usually too late for public opinion to have any effect on policy. Similarly, serious and in-depth analysis of contexts and historical background, and criticism of the motives and potential benefits for certain actors behind decisions to engage in armed conflict, often constitute a negligible portion of content. Thrall (2000) in his detailed study of the White House press strategy during wars (from Vietnam in 1965 to the first Gulf War in 1990) argues that governments and the military would be only too willing to impose direct measures of censorship on the press (including television, which is considered to be the most 'dangerous' medium of all). Thrall (2000: 46–7) says that:

> Presidents fear that even a successful, low-casualty conflict could be ruinous to their political fortunes if television managed to transmit footage of even a few soldiers losing their lives in the wrong way or at the wrong time . . . this fear has motivated the White House to seek greater controls over what the media reports.

It is doubtful that public opinion would be very accommodating if the restriction of information on behalf of the government on important matters, such as conflict or violence, were to become subject to straightforward censorship or blatant 'filtering' of journalists. The methods usually adopted are subtler and are not communicated to the public through the media that the government aims to control. Usually, information about such practices becomes available through the investigative efforts of independent journalists and researchers, sometimes after the crisis is over. Yet, the importance of (and need for) controlling information and content have found quite obvious expression in disagreements between prime ministers and the media over the coverage of strikes, war, investigations into government policy or the conflict in Northern Ireland (Seymour-Ure 1996: 207). An example of the uneasy relationship between government and media is the broadcasting ban issued by the British government between 1987 and 1995, which prohibited broadcasters from providing airtime to certain political parties and groups such as Sinn Fein, the political wing of the Irish Republican Army (IRA). This was justified by the claim that depriving such groups of the 'oxygen of publicity' would serve to reduce violence (Frost 2000: 51–2).

There are other laws that prevent journalists from gathering information: the Official Secrets Act 1989, and the system of 'D notices' that prohibits the reporting of issues characterized as sensitive. However, the problems of war reporting and control of the news do not always take an easily recognizable form. In the second Gulf War, led by George Bush Jr and Tony Blair (in 2003), a large number of journalists and television crews were in place to cover the news for channels that would transmit footage around the world. Embedded journalists, as they were termed (that is, journalists who travelled with the troops), became the rule rather than the exception. The military (both British and American) had 'warned' journalists that their safety could not be guaranteed if they did not attach themselves to the allied troops. Although no one said outright that their reports would be controlled or censored, the outcome was that many journalists had a very limited spectrum of sources from which they could take their 'news', had a limited perception of the broader context of the war and were unable to report from all sides. Those journalists who were not 'embedded' risked their lives to cover the war 'on the ground'; some were killed by 'friendly fire' (Johnson 2003). Reports also mention non-embedded journalists who were unlawfully held, restricted or abused by the military (Rense.com 2003). In any case, embedded journalism raises more questions about the ethics of journalism than the perspectives it claims to cover. Although embedded journalists themselves might not necessarily have felt censored or intimidated in reporting on what they witnessed, it is certainly too strong an argument to ignore that living and working next to soldiers who carry weapons can compromise one's own emotional and ethical well-being. One has no choice but to forge friendships with the military, especially considering that the unarmed journalist's own life may often depend on the protection of these soldiers.

Direct and indirect restrictions on content

The effectiveness of self-regulation, in the form of bodies such as the Press Complaints Commission (PCC), as discussed in a later chapter, is questionable. Indeed, evidence suggests that the effectiveness and regulatory powers of the PCC are minuscule. Petley (1999) argues that the PCC does not desire more powers as this would probably mean increased responsibilities that would require more vigorous scrutiny of the job of the press. Moreover, the chairman of the PCC and most of the press campaigned against the introduction of the European Convention on Human Rights, which guarantees the right to freedom of expression and therefore provides journalists with a real right that can protect them in their attempts to practise better investigative journalism (i.e. asking difficult questions). Although the UK introduced the European Convention on Human Rights in 1998, it will take some time for any substantial effects to become evident. The freedom of journalists to practise investigative journalism is at present restricted by laws that directly prohibit them from seeking certain information, whose protection is justified as being in the interests of national security (as is often claimed in times of armed conflict). This line of reasoning is made by actors who are ultimately unaccountable, since there is no possibility of questioning the correctness of a decision made to label information as potentially harmful to the national interest.

Restrictive laws can have a negative influence on the publication of information by creating an environment where the risks of making oneself subject to legal action (and the costs and time this involves) outweigh journalistic ethics. One such example is that of the law on 'confidence', which was basically intended to protect information on trade secrets but has gradually expanded to the world of the media. The publication of confidential information can be deemed a 'breach of confidence' by the courts. There is no need for a written contract that declares which part of information given – in any form (e.g. photographs or text) – is confidential. One of the main conditions for an act to be deemed as 'breach of confidence' would be the (unfair) publication of information without authorization (Barendt and Hitchens 2000: 389–93). As Petley (1999: 147) notes, the most crucial stage is that of 'interim injunction'. This means that a publication can be stopped until the case of information publishing comes to trial. As with the case of indirect censorship discussed above, by the time a trial gets under way (and there is no guarantee of a decision in favour of the publication), the crucial time has passed and the information in question might have lost its significance. Considering the costly and time-consuming process of reaching a decision, the media may choose not to pursue the matter after all. One of the most controversial elements of 'breach of confidence' cases, however, is the fact that the media involved are not even allowed to report on the 'interim injunction'. Thus there not only remains the problem that potentially useful information is left undisclosed, but also that disclosing any other piece of information regarding the process is also restrained.

London is also known as 'the libel capital of the world' due to the fact that conditions for libel plaintiffs are more favourable there than in any other city in the world. This is mainly because libel law requires defendants (newspapers, broadcasters and, increasingly, Internet service providers) to prove that the information they publish is not defamatory. Second, there is no defence of publication in the 'public interest'. These are conditions that have a restrictive effect on potentially important material, which will not be published by the media for fear (as noted above) of costly and time-consuming processes that tend not to look favourably on publishers. This capacity of the libel law to, effectively, censor output has contributed to an environment of exceptionally high self-censorship in the realm of Internet publications. It is also becoming alarmingly evident in the shutting down of Internet sites on behalf of powerful companies. In these cases, Internet service providers (ISPs) withdraw material even though this material may be in the public interest (Index on Censorship 2002 and *Independent* 2002).

Other measures introduced to control content in the British media are specialist ones directed exclusively at the content of broadcasters. A set of measures is to be found in the internal codes of the BBC, the *Producer's Guidelines*, and the equivalent ITC Programme Code. The press is accountable to the PCC (which replaced the Press Council in 1991) as a response to public demands for some control over the increasingly intrusive character of press stories about the private lives of people in the 'media spotlight'. The Broadcasting Standards Commission has also issued Codes of Guidance, while in the field of video and film the British Board of Film Classification (BBFC) has developed a set of standards for the classification of films divided into categories of age (such as 12, 15, 18, etc.) that correspond to content deemed appropriate to be viewed by audiences of the particular age group. Usually, matters of nudity, sex and violence are considered to be central to this classification policy, although context 'is central to the question of [the] acceptability' of a programme (see BBFC Principles).

The climate of fear in the world of public communications is generated by direct and indirect means. Restricting measures over expression are often claimed to be justified in the name of decency, and the protection of morals and social order; they are even said to be in the public interest. 'Restricting measures' are laws, such as the libel law, that directly restrict expression of opinion, but also conditions that indirectly impose controls over writers and journalists through the exercise of self-censorship. Curran and Seaton (1997), discussing policy directed at the control of media content, divide policy into two major philosophical approaches: legal paternalism and legal libertarianism. Defenders of the former hold that a 'nanny state' should be responsible in defining moral standards as portrayed through the media by strengthening the laws on obscenity and indecency, and effectively extending censorship. A recent survey carried out on behalf of Index on Censorship indicates that,

Table 4.1: Media policy in the UK

Major policy documents	Year	Main recommendations	Politics and society
The British Telecommuni-cations Act	1981	Separated British Telecom from the Post Office; terminated British Telecom's monopoly.	In the UK, Conservative, pro-market government in power. In France socialists in power: monopoly abandoned but extra help given to public service media. Italy: Berlusconi's media in duopoly with RAI.
The 1984 Telecommuni-cations Act	1984	Created Office of Telecom-munications (Oftel) to regulate licences. Initial period of duopoly.	
Broadcasting Act	1990	Independent Television Commission (ITC) to regulate all private services in the UK.	Bush and Yeltsin proclaim a formal end to the Cold War in 1992; HTML as web design; Balkan wars; Clinton (Democrat) president; Clinton–Gore announce the 'infor-mation superhighway'; USA privatizes Internet management; digitization of TV and cameras; in 1997, 69 countries members of the WTO, agree to liberalize communi-cations; BSkyB 200-channel digital satellite service launched (1998); EU single currency plans; deregulation and privatization of public services.
Broadcasting Act	1996	The operation of digital terrestrial television in Britain; cross-ownership and ownership rules allow more concentration. In 1998 the first digital terrestrial channel was launched: BBC Choice using BSkyB as carrier.	
Communica-tions Bill	2002	Ofcom to become the super-regulator over the ITC, the Broadcasting Standards Commission, Oftel, the Radio Authority and the Radiocommunica-tions Agency.	Silvio Berlusconi (media mogul), prime minister of Italy (2001); Bush (Republican) US president by court ruling; 'war on terrorism' led by USA; EU single currency (euro); preparatory conferences of the World Summit on Information Society (WSIS, 2003); NGOs and civil society campaign for the 'Right to Communicate' as a human right.

Source: adapted from PressWise; Frost 2000; **Guardian** Online; ITC, BSC, BBC, PCC and Radio Authority websites although a vast majority of university students (92 per cent) believe that our society is censored, a (smaller) majority (62 per cent) also agree with the idea that the state has to set the limits of censorship (Index on Censorship 2003). The legal libertarian approach argues that freedom of expression should be incorporated in a written constitution and therefore protected. This would mean that a number of restrictions, whether in the form of control over content or control over practices, could be brought to court and would be scrutinized by judges. Although this is not unusual in other European countries (since justice is thought to be an estate independent of the government and with responsibility to ensure that state is not above the law), opponents in Great Britain are not in favour (Curran and Seaton 1997: 351).

With the introduction of the European Convention on Human Rights and Fundamental Freedoms in 1998 (Council of Europe 1950) Great Britain took a step forward in the protection of the right to freedom of expression although, as discussed earlier, other legislation (such as the Official Secrets Act 1989 and libel law) can be seen as undermining the intention of Article 10. It is important to ask the question 'Whom does the policy benefit?' Does it empower individual citizens and social groups to express their opinion and make their material experiences and conditions of living known through the communication media? Or does it benefit actors who already have power and are more likely to influence content, such as persons of high status in decision-making centres, those with enough wealth to afford the legal costs involved in suing misrepresenting media, or the media owners themselves?

Communications Bill 2002: the birth of a super-regulator

At the beginning of the new millennium, the Labour government decided to further the liberalization of the communications market with a new policy initiative introduced within the framework of the Communications Bill (yet to be voted on by the Parliament at the time of writing). According to the new proposed policies, a number of areas will be reformed, in particular those relevant to media ownership and the organization of content-regulating bodies.

The new super-regulator, Ofcom, is replacing the Broadcasting Standards Commission, the Independent Television Commission, Oftel and the Radio Authority. The Radiocommunications Agency will continue to exist as it acts in the name of the Secretary of State. The function of the bodies responsible for content quality in broadcast media is expected to be replaced by a new Content Board, set up by Ofcom, that will introduce new guidelines.

The government has proposed further relaxation of regulation on cross-ownership, most likely to move away from the 20 per cent limit established by the 1996 Broadcasting Act. Although this measure was introduced with Rupert Murdoch in mind (and therefore to protect commercial media from ownership concentration in the hands of one mogul), in 2002 the government said that policy has, this time, been designed with no particular person in mind. Nevertheless, intense criticism of the proposed bill put the government in a position where it had to add new clauses for the protection of content on Five (formerly Channel 5) in case the broadcaster (currently owned by RTL) is bought by, say, News Corporation (*Guardian*, 28 January 2003). Further common ownership of national television and radio will be permitted, while the rule that non-EEA persons are excluded from owning broadcasting licences is to be lifted. Similarly, now, advertising agencies, local authorities and religious bodies will be able to acquire broadcasting licences.

Ofcom will have the right to impose new measures regarding content: it will be able to demand that broadcasters increase their participation in domestic productions, and include these in their programming, if it feels that (cheap) American productions are dominating. Also, further clauses will require that Five invests and commissions the production of programmes at a regional level and therefore outside London, in the same way that the BBC is required to. Ofcom maintains the right to intervene if it deems that the proportion of regionally produced programming is insufficient, thus introducing a quota reserved for special (regional) programming. These measures are referred to as 'public service' obligations.

Ofcom consists of nine members who will make decisions (with a 'light touch' as far as content is concerned) in the, increasingly convergent, media field. One of the novelties introduced in the Communications Bill is the explicit attention given to employment in the media sector as it introduces measures of equal opportunities and employment matters in the media industries. The irony is that within this super-regulator – which concentrates in its hands authority over broadcasting *and* press, content *and* structure, as well as decision-making powers over matters of interest to the (media) industrial world *and* of consumers – only two women hold the position of board member. Another woman is a legal adviser, while the remaining six seats (two-thirds of the board) are occupied by men. Also, the top positions – chairman, deputy chair, chair of the content board and chief executive – are all occupied by men. As far as the effectiveness of this super-regulator goes, only time will tell.

At the time of writing the merger of two ITV companies (Carlton and Granada) into one super-company was made possible despite restrictions on ownership competition. For such a merger to become possible, the government had to give the green light for the merging companies to act in a way that effectively meant defeating the competition rules of 'fair' game. The advertising sector in particular was quick to point out that the concentration of control over the audience market will set a problematic framework, within which 'fair' competition cannot take place. The fears that advertisers express relate specifically to the merging of the advertising sales arms of the television companies. The combination of both advertising sales divisions means greater control over the amount of time and the costs of advertising on the new super-company's channels.

Conclusions

Media policy covers a wide spectrum of media activities and communication processes. These involve the structural changes of the media system in Great Britain, and the terms of competition and access to the media. Policies also address problems arising from the nature of certain kinds of programming, such as those containing sex and violence. Audiences, and the suitability of programming for certain audiences, have also become objects of regulation through the establishment and operation of forms of censorship or 'preventative' regulation issuing guidelines and notices according to the age of the prospective audience (BBFC) or to the nature of the content (D-notices). There is strong criticism of major areas of media policy, in particular those that fail to protect some necessary degree of pluralism of sources and those that involve the policing of content, whether direct or indirect. It is argued that restrictive policies often hinder the smooth operation of the media and their democratic role of exercising the right to criticize the government (the right to information), whereas in other cases censorship is indirectly applied through conditions imposed on the media to prevent them from reporting on certain cases (mostly as a result of the 'breach of confidence' policy).

FURTHER READING

(Repeated from Chapter 3)

Jäckel, A. (2003) *European Film Industries*, London: bfi: Chapter 4.
A comprehensive chapter discussing in great detail production strategies and policies in Europe. Major policy initiatives are referred to as is their impact on European production, within which the reader can place the UK position in a comparative setting.

McPherson, C. (2000) Death to the Entrepreneur: an Examination of the Use of Technology and Legislation to Control Programme Piracy at the Dawn of the Digital Era. In Lees, T., Ralph, S. and Langham Brown, J. (eds), *Is Regulation Still an Option in a Digital Universe?* Luton: University of Luton Press.
The chapter examines practices of piracy in relation to digital satellite television and, in particular, access to programmes. It discusses the policy initiatives taken and considered by the EU in that respect and makes reference to the entrepreneurial losses suffered.

Reading, A. (1999) Campaigns to Change the Media. In Stokes, J. and Reading, A. (eds), *Media in Britain: Debates and Developments*, London: Macmillan.
This chapter offers a comprehensive discussion of the ideological and cultural underpinnings of cultural and media policy, and the organized attempts of the public to change the media. The author divides such attempts into three categories: those that relate to media morality, those with the aim of achieving greater participation on the part of the public, and those that address discriminatory media practices against certain groups of people.

chapter five

The role of the public

Until now, we have discussed a number of aspects of the British media system. The study of the history, policy and structure of the media is helpful in identifying a number of influential actors, patterns and tendencies that define the cultural products delivered and circulated by the media. But to whom are these products distributed? Until now, we have discussed the role of international policy, the influence of historically traceable conditions (such as the development of international trade and military dominance) that shape the forms of media available today, the role of technology and the market, as well as the role of the state in defining the ideological principles on which media systems are called to base their function in British society. However, it is also important to ask questions about the role of the people who receive the meanings, messages and products as, after all, without audiences, without receivers who are able to understand and make their own meanings, media products lose their significance.

Equally, without a social context made by commonly accepted or dominating beliefs, no product has any meaning, no matter how well presented it is. Who comprises the public that is called to consume the products made available by the media industry? Are audiences anything more than simple consumers? Are they located at the very end of the production–dissemination process continuum as passive receivers, or do they play an active role in the interpretation of the meanings and products they receive? Are the audiences involved in any way in the production of messages? Are citizens active participants in the formation of policy that defines media operations? Is the protection of the public good an objective? In other words, do we have any role to play at all?

The public: one or many?

Often, references to 'the public' are made as if that public were one homogeneous and undifferentiated entity. Treating the public as a great mass has mainly to do with ideological representations of the public that serve specific goals, such as the creation of national identity. So, for example, in the case of the Falklands War, when then Prime Minister Margaret Thatcher told the BBC to refer to the British armed forces as '*our* forces', there were at least two ideological components at work. First, by the use of 'our' the BBC was called to take sides and present the war as a matter for the whole 'nation'. Second, in order to do this, it was necessary that representations made in a public domain – such as the BBC television news –

only recognized a homogeneous *imagined community*. Furthermore, constructions based on 'we' and 'they' further reinforce the construction of imagined communities, such as the nation.

'Imagined community' is a term introduced by Anderson in his influential work of 1983, *Imagined Communities*. Anderson's thesis emphasizes the processes through which the sense of community, national or cultural, is constructed. These processes are predominantly based on the sense of shared goals and origins: cultural, geographical, linguistic or other. At the same time, the coherence of these communities is dependent on traits that are constructed and imagined. For example, nations are broadly based on assumptions of superiority over other nations or ideas of patriotism. As Anderson says (1983: 15–16), imagined communities are imagined because people will never know most of their fellow community members,

> yet in the minds of each lives the image of their communion ... the nation is imagined as a community because, regardless of the actual inequality and exploitation that may prevail in each, the nation is always conceived as a deep, horizontal comradeship.

Schlesinger (1991) further discusses the idea of imagined community to emphasize that homogeneity is a different issue from community and 'comradeship'. Homogeneity need not be prearranged or pre-existent. As a matter of fact, homogeneity within communities and publics is something that is actively constructed. It is therefore not a static trait or an accomplished fact (Schlesinger 1991: 164). This is where the producers of cultural artefacts and meanings play an active and significant role. The construction of homogeneity involves a series of strategies, one of which is the example mentioned at the beginning of this chapter, with the silencing of opposition.

National communities are of course not the only collective communities that are addressed by the media or to whom cultural products and meanings are directed. The public consists of diverse social groups who do not share equal power within society. Collective communities other than national ones are also present. They may occupy different places within, or spaces beyond, the national community, as is the case with international networks and professional communities. The members of lesbian and gay communities can, for example, be members of national, cultural or political communities simultaneously. A number of socioeconomic factors determine the position of social groups. Class, gender, race, age and even sexuality are structural determinants that become a significant part of the basis on which people form communities, socialize, interact and interpret media products. These socioeconomic factors are important in the cultivation of preferences for specific cultural products, taste, lifestyle, or political and religious beliefs. Furthermore, such factors determine to a significant extent the relation of publics to the media. They are important not only in determining the degree of access to media products and information resources, but also influential in terms of the use of media, whether it be television, newspapers or the Internet.

Socioeconomic inequalities and differentiated socialization within publics in countries of similar economic and political systems, such as those of western Europe, are enough to form the basis according to which a number of choices are made. For example the *Guardian*'s target audience is middle-class university graduates of the centre-left, while *The Times*' readership is drawn mainly from the middle class with centre-right political affiliations. However, even when people consume the same media products, as in the case of a soap opera, their interpretation of the content can be significantly different. These differences in interpretation are related to the personal and social experiences of people as individuals, but also as members of social groups. A process of 'contextualizing' takes place every time we consume media products – that is, we work with the meanings and place them within familiar contexts of our social experience and knowledge, defined by factors such as social and economic status, level of education, gender, age and race (Burch 2002).

The 'public' is, therefore, more than a homogenized mass that likes, needs or believes in the same things. The media industries have capitalized on these differences and to a significant extent have also cultivated them in order to create and feed media markets. The expansion of the specialist press is a typical example of this.

Those aspects of differentiation of the public that are based on imbalances of power and social inequality are, however, used further by the media. Social stereotypes, prejudices and ideologies that seek to naturalize inequalities and provide justification for inferiority of sex, race, nations and people, but also the unequal distribution of wealth and power, are some of the factors responsible for the unequal treatment of members of the public. Examples of this are the lack of interest shown by the mainstream media with regard to representing conflicting views, the stories of ordinary people or works dealing with peace. Furthermore, the access of the public to the production of meanings is also unequal. Meanings circulated by the media are not produced by audiences but by specific elites, such as experts, writers, journalists and producers. From a Marxist point of view, the interests of these elites are not identical to those of the public. It is argued that, often, these elites (including the owners of the media) have different and even conflicting interests from the public's. The private or commercial media are interested in making a profit, an objective that is not always compatible with the production of difficult and/or unpopular content. It is therefore reasonable to argue that the public as a whole is made up of publics that do not necessarily share the same values even though they inhabit the same national boundaries. It is therefore important to take into account such possible differentiations of the public and acknowledge that a discussion about 'the public' may actually entail an understanding of 'the publics'. This highly contested term can perhaps be understood better, and may be put to better use, if we consider the different qualities and roles of the public in relation to the media production process and regulation. The following discussion identifies these roles.

The public as audience

The discussion of the power of media messages in society is often associated with the question of the powerlessness of the receivers of messages, pointing to the idea of passive masses. Media and sociological theories often treat media communication as a one-way process, with clear and distinctive boundaries of sender, message and receiver. In this process, the receivers of messages are in a disadvantaged position compared to the senders, as they do not participate in the creation of meaning. Senders, or producers, are in control of the nature, form, content and length of messages; they reach large audiences and they have the power to lead, direct, legitimize or silence public opinion. The receiving masses therefore have little control over the production and dissemination of media messages. It is the critical theorists that identify the publics as passive, weak or simply in a position of no control over public communication as facilitated by the mass media. Liberal theory, on the other hand, views the media as the 'fourth estate', an agent with the power and function to question authority and provide a plurality of information sources for the public. The ideas and limitations of such approaches are discussed in relation to the public as consumers.

An extremely influential school of thought was put forward by the Frankfurt School. Theodor Adorno, Max Horkheimer, Walter Benjamin, Leo Loewenthal and Herbert Marcuse are some of the most representative critical theorists of this school whose work has brought the dynamics of capitalism, media production, audiences and politics to the forefront of media debates. Although there are significant differences between Benjamin's and Adorno's respective approaches to mass media and audiences, it is reasonable to say that the Frankfurt School treats the media as significant players in the formation of public opinion. Having witnessed the fall of the Weimar Republic and the rise of the Nazi regime, these German theorists paid particular attention to the influence of media propaganda on society's desensitization to totalitarianism. Central to their argument is the assumption that the media reproduce and reinforce the ideologies of dominant political and/or economic groups in society. Systematic representation of the interests of dominant groups allows, therefore, very little space for the articulation of alternative meanings. As Lippman's (1930) classic study on public opinion and media propaganda revealed, the media do not just mirror or reflect society, they are active in the creation of a particular idea of society through the means of propaganda. Of course, Lippman was talking about direct, predominantly state, propaganda in the first half of the century. Since then, studies of the interpretative ability of audiences have brought an added perspective to the analysis of the public's relation to media messages.

Research into the public's relation to the media has also indicated that audiences are not simply the passive receivers some theorists claim them to be. Audiences do play an active part in the deconstruction and interpretation of media messages. The 'active audience' is a term that Croteau and Hoynes (2000) apply to signify the importance of human agency. They identify three categories of audience responsiveness to media: individual interpretation of meanings, collective interpretation and collective political action. Individual interpretation is the activity of making sense of a message, giving it a meaning and placing it within a context. This is not an independent process. It is based on our prior knowledge and understanding of the world within which individuals are called to assign meanings to images, sounds and words. Human societies construct language as part of their communication systems. This language, which is not limited to the written word but can also be visual or in some other form, conveys meanings attached to words through a system of conventions. If we have never seen and do not know what a book is, the word 'book' alone will not be enough to help us understand the object we are talking about. Similarly, if we are knowledgeable about the object and its name, 'book', but we are not aware of the fact that there are other forms of written passages, organized in the form of magazines, then, although we understand what a book is, it is difficult to imagine any other organization of texts. In other words, it is more difficult to assign meanings to things that are not available to us through prior knowledge.

In order for science fiction to make sense to audiences it is based on issues that deal with realities we have already learned to recognize. For example, an episode of *Star Trek* deals with issues that are basic to human societies, such as conflict, science, interpersonal relationships. A battle between the Star Ship *Voyager* and a Borg cube symbolizes the ideological conflict between individualism and absolute communality. At a different level, it may be understood to refer to the principles of western capitalist societies based on individualism against what was seen to be the totalitarian organization of communist societies, or other forms of organization of social life that are a threat to capitalist individualism. It can also be argued that the Star Ship *Voyager* represents the future United States, transformed into a federation of planets (where all species speak English!), and the supremacy of American militarism in its role of exploration. (All *Star Trek* series – the original series, *Next Generation, Deep Space Nine, Voyager* – were being shown on four different channels on British TV, Sky One, Sky Mix, BBC2 and E4, at the time of writing.)

The dominant theme of the series is, of course, science. The very idea that only science gives the right answers is a highly ideological standpoint, as is the idea that science is objective. Science as the ultimate truth is used in the series to explain what we now consider fantastic and unreal. The strangest situations find an explanation through scientific jargon, which makes sense within the context of the world in which the crew of *Voyager* lives. The basic principles of this world are easily understood by a variety of heterogeneous audiences around the world. Some of the dominant values of western societies (or the establishment) are present in this science fiction series. These are the prominence of exploration and science, wars between planets (replacing wars between nations), hierarchy of command, personalizations of reason and logic (in the fictional person of Tuvok) or uncontrollable anger, humanity as a quality already in the possession of the heroines and heroes or as a quality for which holograms or humanoids (the doctor in *Voyager*, Commander Data in *Next Generation*) strive to achieve, good and evil, and individualism as the highest quality of all. Thus, although the programme deals with fictional situations, placed in a distant future (the twenty-fourth century), it still relies on language, text conventions and familiar social relations, such as hierarchy or heterosexuality. It therefore utilizes patterns of which audiences can make sense. The series is not British, in that it was not made in Great Britain, by British companies, but one of the main protagonists was British (Captain Picard). It is, however, highly successful in Britain and can be 'read' by Britons and others residing in Britain in a variety of different ways.

Texts like this one are 'open' in that they allow interpretation according to cultural background and other socioeconomic characteristics. They can appeal to national as well as international audiences. *Star Trek*, a US production, is a text open enough to be followed by very diverse audiences around the world. This doesn't necessarily mean that all audiences create the same meanings. But nor does it mean that the number of interpretations is unlimited.

In their study of international audiences' interpretation of US soap operas, Liebes and Katz (1993) found significant differences among cultures. The study indicated that each ethnic group studied (Americans, Japanese and Russian, Moroccan, Arab and kibbutz communities in Israel) concentrated on different aspects of the soap opera in question

(*Dallas*). Arabs and Moroccan Jews were more likely to recall the scene sequence of the episode they watched; Russians concentrated on the message of the programme; while Americans concentrated on the traits of the characters' personalities. This does not show that ethnic communities are predestined to interpret messages in a specific way. On the contrary, it demonstrates that culture, and therefore socialization and material dynamics, are the defining factors of audiences' interpretation. This example also demonstrates the limited range of understandings and interpretations of a text. These again depend on class, gender and cultural background. Research has shown that the middle classes have different perceptions of the media from the working classes. Press (1991) found that women from the middle classes did not attach any sense of 'realism' to television and were more likely to treat televised images of women with distrust. Working-class women, on the other hand, understood depictions of middle-class women as realistic portrayals. Furthermore, working-class women dismissed popular images of women, while middle-class women concentrated on the positive aspects of these images. As Press (1991) and Croteau and Hoynes (2000) in their discussion emphasize, middle-class women tend to be less aware of questions of class than working-class women. As they also come from the same socioeconomic group as the television producers (middle class) they tend to find the roles of women 'normal'.

Morley (1980) in his study of audiences' responses to the *Nationwide* news magazine programme also showed that there are strong indications that the interpretation of meanings depends on social and economic positions that people occupy. Although, as he says, class does not *determine* the way we interpret media messages, it does play an important role. This is related to the tools available to audiences to accept, negotiate or oppose media messages, by accepting the 'preferred reading' of these messages or by creating oppositional meanings. In order to do the latter, however, audiences need to have additional 'tools', such as information sources, that will allow them to question the preferred reading. Morley's study found that bank managers' reading of a programme about economic affairs was in accordance with the preferred reading of the text. He found that bank managers and programme producers projected the same views about the economy. Workers, however, found the programme one-sided, favouring the views of bank managers. Because workers had experience of trade unions, they had access to a set of 'tools' that allowed their opposition to the preferred meaning. As bank managers and producers belong to the same class, they regarded the coverage of economic issues as realistic.

Ross's studies (1997; 2001) of the representation of people with disabilities in the media reinforce the evidence that audiences can critically respond to media messages, especially when depictions or representations do not respond to the way people understand themselves to be. For example, disabled people in Britain expressed distrust and anger about television portrayals of disability. One of the main points made by the audiences in these studies was the fact that neither media producers, actors nor presenters had the necessary experience of ill-health or disability to provide realistic depictions or produce useful and truthful programmes. Such misrepresentations are widely thought, however, to be accurate, and therefore reinforce further a polarization among the public, between 'us' (able-bodied) and 'them' (disabled). Similarly, stereotyping and the polarization of mediated images and messages alienate parts of the audience in relation to others.

These studies help us understand some of the dynamics of active interpretation of media messages. They all address the dynamics of class, gender and race in the deconstruction of meanings. Furthermore, they demonstrate how structural determinants restrict people's 'active agency' in the process (Croteau and Hoynes 2000: 23). Philo and Miller (2001: 50–1), criticizing the assumption that media messages mean different things to different people and that texts are infinitely open to a diversity of interpretations, point out the nature of differences between groups. These are not differences between groups over the meaning of the message but over 'whether they believed it or not'. Philo and Miller, too, emphasize the role of pre-existing beliefs, direct experience and knowledge of the subject represented or covered.

At the same time, it is important to remember that the media industries construct audiences for two main purposes: to create and sustain a market for their own products, and to 'sell' these audiences to advertisers. The production process would be too risky for media industries if their audiences were unpredictable and unknown. Business would be difficult with an unknown customer. Therefore, market and audience research makes sure that the audiences are constructed in categories that are easy to identify, and according to which a specific set of programmes can be produced. As Gitlin (1994) emphasizes, although these first categorizations do not represent reality, because the pictures of the public are partial and can change over time, they serve as the basis for the production of media goods. The reinforcement of these programmes serves to 'control' possible differentiations of the public. Media production in this sense – working with a specific, even 'ideal', type of audience in mind – 'tames' its audience and 'educates' it into accepting the produced cultural artefacts. This in turn means that the media industry can maintain its audiences over time (for example, through soap operas or a set of products that the audience has learnt to understand and accept, such as talk shows, and game shows like *Blind Date* or *Who Wants to Be a Millionaire?*). The next step is for the companies to sell their audiences to the advertisers. This way, when advertisers sponsor a programme or buy advertising time on a channel or space in a newspaper, they buy access to a specific part of the public. The presentation of the advertising products will already have been adequately modified in order to appeal to the 'trained' public they address. A useful test of this might be to examine the advertisement of travel and related industries in the *Sun* and in the *Guardian*, and compare the two. It would be interesting to examine how the travel industry presents itself to its potential customers, the differences and similarities in advertising between these newspapers and the relationship to the rest of the content (news, feature articles, etc.).

The active public and the interactive medium: Britain on-line

Ordinary members of the public rarely ever determine the content of the media they consume. As consumers, our active role is limited to making choices between pre-manufactured goods listed in our TV or radio guide, or the books available on the shelves of bookstores and supermarkets. Of course, there has always been some form of interactivity with the media we consume. We have always had the option to switch off our radio, change the television channel, stop buying a magazine or switch to a different newspaper. We have also had the option to read certain articles and ignore others, we have been able to use the commercial break in films or between programmes to do other things and use other media, such as calling or texting a friend. However, we have probably participated in other ways: we may have sent a complaint to a TV channel or entered our names in a newspaper competition, voted for our favourite pop star or telephoned a programme to express our opinion. Media have often offered different avenues for enabling some form of a two-way communication with the public.

However, none of these methods or media has ever delivered what the Internet promises to offer: an unlimited world of interaction where consumers can search for and find information, entertainment, business and even education. The promises of the digital and on-line revolution extend to all spheres of life, offering interactivity, action and borderlessness of time and space. Perhaps one of the most typical expressions of the Internet 'hype' can be seen in the commercial promotion of the former British (now part of the French company Wanadoo), Internet provider Freeserve: its campaign utilizes images of the 1960s, the hippy subculture and peace movements to advertise subscription to its 24-hour Internet access at a flat rate. This service is advertised as an example of 'freedom', where one can go anywhere, anytime, free from the time restrictions of dial-up services and costs per minute. Certainly, few things are really free in our economic system, so this 'freedom' comes with a monthly cost of approximately £15 (about 50p a day), which is a little less than the daily wage of a sweatshop worker in the developing world. In the UK, 52 per cent of the adult population has access to the Internet, the highest proportions being in the east of England (52 per cent) and London (50 per cent). However, of households with a low income, only 10 per cent can afford an Internet connection, compared with 82 per cent of those households with a high income (NUA 2002). The data show a clear trend: the Internet, the medium of freedom, is available to those parts of the population that can afford it. Access to information and content, as well as the hardware necessary, along with the skills needed to work with the new medium and process the information available, are important factors that determine the use of the Internet.

Despite these problems, predictions about the growth of broadband adoption in Europe place the UK second after Germany by 2006 (NUA 2003a). This wonder medium is clearly *the* medium of the (post-)industrialized world: Europe is home to 23 per cent of the world's Internet users, while the USA accounts for almost one-third. Latin America accounts for only 2 per cent (NUA 2003b). These figures illustrate the unequal distribution of the Internet and highlight the fact that debates surrounding the potential of the Internet should be attended to with this inequality in mind. Some of the issues related to the potential of the Internet for democratization and decentralization of services, or the emphasis on empowerment of the 'end user' are not necessarily relevant to the material conditions of Sub-Saharan Africa, for example. The dominance of the western world in terms of the communications infrastructure, software and content, represents priorities and interests that do not necessarily tally with the concerns of the majority of people in the world, who live on less than $1 a day. What this tells us is that the issues we address here are probably specific and relevant mainly to the prosperous – *minority* – parts of the world.

Interactivity has become an important issue because it refers to the idea that through the participation of the public, the democratization of the media is possible. It also implies that audiences are active. Implications of what constitutes 'interactivity', are thought to fall predominantly into three areas: consumers can archive and recirculate media content; DIY cultures are born of audiences who create their own content; finally, the industrial trend of horizontal media ownership provides a complex multimedia system that demands 'more active modes of spectatorship' (Jenkins 2002: 157).

These 'active modes of spectatorship' can be exercised at websites such as that linked to the TV reality show *Big Brother*, on-line games or interactive quizzes. Some websites claim that they 'do not work unless you work them' (*Big Brother*), inviting the participation of the viewer-user in choosing and adding links, and reading and adding comments or news to the site. Most Internet providers, or portals, will encourage users to create their own websites or customize their homepage. Most companies have constructed their own websites where further interaction can take place through the purchasing of goods, watching movie trailers or participating in discussion fora.

Very early on, the Internet was associated with free content. Content is still provided free of charge. In Britain, subscription fees have not proved to be popular, as the *Financial Times*' FT.Com case demonstrated when only 17,000 of its 3 million readers subscribed to its on-line version (Curran and Seaton 2003: 281). One of the most frequently visited sites, the on-line version of the newspaper, the *Guardian*, has introduced a different system to encourage customers to pay a subscription fee. The site offers a subscription service to the on-line version of the newspaper, which is free from advertising. In the free on-line version of the *Guardian*, the text is surrounded by advertisements that change constantly. The *Guardian*, although creator of one of the most successful websites, operates its site in the same way as those of other papers, such as the *Sun*, *FT* or *Times*, and depends on its print version for on-line content. The difference is that these on-line versions can host discussion fora and live chats available to registered users. The *Guardian* site also contains a searchable archive and an expanded set of weblogs (diary-like entries and listings of other websites carrying relevant information about a variety of aspects related to a specific topic). For example, coverage of the possible re-election of George W. Bush and the issues related to his presidency and policy are addressed in a dedicated weblog under the title 'US Vote 2004' (www.guardian.co.uk/weblog/usa/0, 13960,1057810,00.html).

This is one of the many ways in which already established media use the Internet not only to expand the content provided in their conventional form, but also to invite some minimum level of reader interactivity. Similarly, companies modify products to make them suitable for Internet usage, such as on-line games based on films, television series or video games. Interactivity in these cases is expressed through the participation in the game and, in the case of reality TV shows, the users have the opportunity to 'direct' a camera and therefore 'control' the viewing angle of the content. Pornographic sites, some deriving from television channels such as Adult TV or media conglomerates with publications such as *Penthouse* and a number of e-pornography outlets as well, offer the same degree of interactivity where users can type in and 'direct' the activities shown via webcams. Pornography – which is a problematic term and one that should not be used simply to describe sexually explicit material – is probably one of the main winners in the Internet revolution.

So, as we have seen, there are several degrees of interactivity, which are achieved in a variety of ways. The Internet seems to offer the highest degree of interactivity, allowing the convergence of technologies in one medium and 'encouraging' users to utilize different tools.

Masses, consumers, citizens: some thoughts about the public

It is occasionally indicated to us that we are apparently setting out to give the public what we think they need – and not what they want, but few know what they want, and very few what they need. . . . In any case it is better to over-estimate the mentality of the public, than to under-estimate it.

(Reith 1924: 34 in Hutchison 1999a)

The term 'masses' has generally been used as a derogatory term that implies uneducated and uncultured sub-humans compared with well-educated, powerful elites. 'Masses', however, has not always meant inferior human beings; instead, in Marxist terminology, 'masses' are referred to as the combined experience and will of individuals that become the moving force behind social change. Masses have a progressive character.

Early broadcasting history was very much shaped by the assumption that broadcasting, due to its role as an educator, had a separate and very serious function in society: to give the public productions of the highest quality and standards for which decisions were taken by boards and committees whose members had little to do with the 'masses'. Nevertheless, the aspiration to turn 'bewildered' masses into discussants of high culture might have been honourable, but it was also paternalistic and misguided, to say the least. The first 'mission statement' of the BBC openly referred to the father-knows-best policy of the corporation in the selection of programmes. More often than not, though, father's choices for the alienated worker-masses of industrialized Britain hardly ever reflected the issues that were of any real importance to people's real lives. As discussed in Chapter 1, the interwar period was an era characterized by great activity of the social movements in British society and Europe. The General Strike, recession, opposing ideological fronts of totalitarian regimes in Europe, votes for women, the fall of the British Empire were not regarded as important issues to be discussed by the official channels of British media public sphere (which was filled with royal images that had little relevance to the lives of the majority of the people).

Time and again it is apparent that it is due to these social movements and the mobilization of the masses that criticism of a variety of issues has taken place. It was the suffragette movement that fought for and earned women's right to vote, the workers' movements and the strength of the trade unions that demanded better pay, and health and safety at work. These are things we take for granted today, but there are other issues that need to be fought for, issues on which the media do not always report. Similarly, we have experienced at least a century of the oppositional media public sphere, demonstrated through a radical press that criticized governments and facilitated communication among the masses. One form of such communication is the leaflets and newsletters, radical newspapers and other material usually distributed in demonstrations, among trade unions or during direct civil action, such as the attempted blocking of the construction of new motorways in southern England, or activism for the protection of the environment or animal rights.

Certainly, today, it would be difficult for any broadcasting company to openly make statements about the inferiority of the masses and the superiority of the broadcaster, least of all because this would be an insult to its customers and therefore likely to adversely affect its profits. Indeed, private broadcasters such as Sky or Five (formerly Channel 5) tend to 'invite' the participation of the public through reality shows, phone-in programmes and shows that convey the message that broadcasters value public opinion.

In the early days of British broadcasting, however, the ideal of public service broadcasting was conceived in its responsibility to cater for the 'public good'. For this reason, the role of broadcaster was considered too important to be trusted to the hands of the corporate world. The press, of course, has always either been privately owned (by lords or the bourgeoisie) or by organizations representing the politics of the masses (political, radical, party, citizens' groups), which meant that the state never had the same control over the press that it had over broadcasting in Britain. The fact that broadcasting was regarded as too important to be led by the state does not necessarily mean that governments have always served the interests of the public good. Both the monarchy and the government routinely addressed the Empire during the 1920s and 1930s; the Queen continued to refer to the Empire until the early 1960s (MacKenzie 1984). Broadcasts were not designed to address issues of public concern nor to educate or inform citizens. They were designed to convey the message that all was well in the Empire, and to demonstrate commercial and military domination. As MacKenzie notes (1984: 93), these broadcasts were stripped of any reference to controversial issues and were structured to convey a self-congratulatory view of the Empire to the public. Similarly, in the 1950s and 1960s very little content paid attention to, or even acknowledged, the existence of black people in Britain and their rights as citizens. Black people were invisible on British television, as were other marginalized groups in British society, who were portrayed in stereotypical ways and using negative imagery (Ross 1996).

Despite this phenomenal ignorance, the role of the broadcast media, even after the introduction of commercial television (ITV), was perceived to be a social one. In Britain, Lord Reith's vision of the BBC was to educate the populace. Part of this vision was to create media structures that would be equally accessible and universally reachable. The realization of this desire was, however, overshadowed by the fact that the PSB authorities were neither able to surpass, nor were they interested in doing so, their own social, economic and cultural background. The BBC was more interested in high quality standards than in 'pluralism' (Stevenson 2000: 78). In this process, regional programming and the inclusion of popular culture came quite late in the history of the BBC. As such, the south-east was mainly in charge of operations, excluding contributions from other parts of the country.

As Stevenson (2000) notes, the working classes have been more loyal followers of 'independent' television than they have of the BBC, which has attracted predominantly middle-class audiences. For this reason the BBC was soon viewed as a white, male, middle-class institution. As we have seen, women's work, at least in the early days of the BBC, was not recognized. Broadcasting committees and the management of the corporation remain predominantly white and male to this day. Although changes have taken place, these are still far from adequate in terms of creating and promoting a more equal culture. The inadequacy of the BBC in coming closer to the working classes created a gap, or 'niche market', for commercial programming from the regions and independent television. This 'weakness' was one of the main factors that contributed to the popularity of ITV. Here, though, we need to be sceptical about employing linear cause-and-effect logic: the fact that commercial television has become more popular with the working classes does not mean that the sum of the programmes broadcast, mostly sensationalized and tabloidized, are those that the working classes would have created had they been given the means and opportunity to do so. Nor does it necessarily mean that these are the primary preferences of the working classes. As discussed earlier, people's interpretation of media messages depends on a number of factors. It does suggest, however, that the direction of programming might be more appealing to these social strata.

Such suggestions can more easily be understood if we also consider the reasons why people use the media and the ways in which they use them. For example, Radway's 1984 study of the reading habits of middle-class housewives and mothers reveals that this particular group uses romance novels (a culturally devalued artefact and generally not the kind of literature one would expect to find in the reading habits of the middle classes) in a particular way. Radway (1984) found that women were using this kind of material for reasons other than intellectual stimulation. These reasons were identified as escape, time for one's self, fulfilment of emotional needs that cannot be satisfied by their roles as wives or mothers and domesticity, and a temporary refusal to participate in traditional gender roles. It is possible that some sectors of the working classes use commercial television in a similar way.

This disassociation of the PSBs from the needs of the majority of the public proved useful in the development of commercial broadcasting. The situation was intensified in the era of deregulation. The preparation for the privatization of the airwaves and the liberalization of the media market under the Tory government in the late 1980s depended on a rhetoric constructed around the rights and freedom of customers to shop around for and consume media goods of their own choosing. Although the experience was the same in the rest of Europe – that is, liberalization – each national broadcaster had its own 'weak spot' of which the market took advantage. In Greece, for example, the word used for private broadcasting was 'free', a symbolic attribute to demonstrate the difference between the new, and at the time promising, commercial broadcasters as opposed to the state-controlled ones (Sarikakis 2000). Excessive control over broadcasters and, in particular, news bulletins, as well as the recent experience (1967–73) of dictatorship, had left its mark on the national memory. The private broadcasters exploited this problematic relationship of the PSBs with the Greek public and built on an image of independent and unbiased news coverage to win over audiences. The new broadcasters, far from unbiased, were particularly aligned to party politics; moreover, 'free' media, far from independent, are owned by press moguls and other industrialists. In Germany, media liberalization came with the fall of the Berlin Wall and the country's unification. In the developed capitalist part of the country, 'free TV' signalled the triumph of capitalism, the extension of the market to media productions for screen and radio. For the former East Germany, it meant programmes free from state control.

This turn, however, brought with it a change in rhetoric. The central idea(l) of citizens was replaced by customer sovereignty in the philosophy that was behind European broadcasting. In this new era, states and industrialists were in need of solid ground on which to build their empires. This is the ground of legitimacy, a justification for the need for private broadcasters and the break-up of the public monopoly. Liberalization brought different promises in different countries, depending on their national and cultural backgrounds, but the common keywords of this period were 'pluralism' and the rights of 'consumers'. As Humphreys (1996) argues, the *ideological* challenge to the public service broadcasting system was very important for the establishment of private media enterprises. PSB paternalism was counter-argued with freedom of choice, state intervention with freedom of the market, and customer choice expressed as the choice of the audiences became cause for disagreement. Finally, the new technologies could be disseminated more efficiently and the needs of the customers served better through media systems operating in free markets. Against the slowness of the public service monopoly, private interests juxtaposed the need for flexibility and promptness, possible only through a free market. The centrality of citizens in policy documents and public rhetoric gave way to the public in its capacity as customer. PSBs remain, at least theoretically, bound to their responsibilities to citizenry while commercial media are more interested in their relationship with their customers.

The public and the regulators: interventions on content

In Britain, the relationship of the public and the press is not a straightforward one. As Frost (2000: 227) points out, countries that protect the freedom of expression and freedom of the press are more likely to actively protect the rights of their citizens. In Britain, the freedom of the press is not constitutionally protected and neither is the public's freedom of expression, compared to the situation in other countries. Italy, for example, is particularly sensitive to the protection of personal honour, the rights of the citizen and the rights of ownership of one's own image. In many cases a newspaper cannot publish the photograph of a person unless it has been given permission to do so. At the same time, the law enforces the right of journalists to protect their sources and the right not to disclose them. Italy and France also have legislation in place to protect their citizens' privacy. Britain, along with Sweden and the Netherlands, does not have any such laws. Personal 'honour' enjoys no protection in Britain: there are no codes of ethics about personal honour in the UK and the only course of action available is to sue on grounds of defamation of character. Quite the opposite is the case in most European countries, where plagiarism, malicious misrepresentation, calumny, slander, libel and unfounded accusations are regarded as professional offences (Frost 2000: 234–5).

Without any substantial support, the public is restricted in its options for addressing inaccuracy and unfairness in the media. One of the major British traditions, however, seems to be in particularly good use: writing letters of complaint. The public can complain about media standards and content to a number of agencies, depending on the media form.

Complaints (until December 2003, when Ofcom, the new 'super-regulator', took over) could be sent to:

- the Press Complaints Commission (PCC) for cases in newspapers, magazines and periodicals, nationally and regionally
- the Broadcasting Standards Commission (BSC) for cases of unfairness and invasion of privacy in all broadcasting media
- the Independent TV Commission (ITC) in connection with content in breach of the Programme Code
- the Radio Authority in connection with broadcasts that are unfair, inaccurate and offensive
- the Radiocommunications Agency, which deals with complaints about radio interference and pirate radio.

The BBC has a separate complaints service, which deals exclusively with BBC domestic and world services and content. Table 5.1 provides a comparative view of the most important media bodies to whom the public can address their complaints. Yet, the widespread culture of complaint letters does not guarantee any legal protection of the citizen, nor does it guarantee that any formally recognized action will be taken. The system is quite unpredictable, in that the power to follow up any complaint lies with the body to which the complaint has been sent.

The organization of the overseeing bodies in the British media system offers media audiences the opportunity to address issues they find problematic, and encourages them to expect that the authorities and the media will deal with them effectively and within a reasonably short period of time. Although the opportunity to intervene, mainly in matters of content, exists, there are a number of problems with the system. From the comparison of these different bodies it becomes clear that a number of conditions must first be met in order for a complaint made by the public to have any effect on content or the structure of the industry. A complaint seldom results in change. Some particular issues are of interest here. First, the media industry would prefer not to apologize in public and would wish to avoid any admission that mistakes have been made in their reports, not least because of the perceived/possible damage this could do to their image. Nevertheless, press and broadcasters try to resolve issues quickly, especially when there is a direct guideline from the authority in charge of the codes under which they operate. Moreover, for a complaint to have a chance to be upheld by the authorities, it must be made within a particular time-frame, providing all necessary details about the object for which the complaint is being made, *and* the person making the complaint must identify the exact area where the breach of conduct took place.

It is not enough, therefore, simply to complain about a particular scene that in your opinion is degrading to women or people with disabilities; it is also necessary to name the exact guideline that was infringed. Given that many such 'unpleasantnesses' do not correspond to any official guideline, it is highly unlikely that a change in policy will take place to correct the unfairness. Such was the case of an article published by the *Daily Star* on 31 August 2003, where the newspaper accused the Somalian refugee community of having stolen nine donkeys. The newspaper based (or justified) its accusations on the (false) assumption that donkey meat is a Somalian delicacy. The Press Complaints Commission (PCC) is currently investigating this story after a Somalian person (living in England) complained about the inaccuracy, as donkey eating is forbidden in Somalia under Islamic law. The complaints about the damage that such stories cause to the image of whole groups of people, and in this case the particularly vulnerable groups of immigrants and asylum-seekers, in British public opinion were rejected by the PCC. The justification was that there is no clause that is meant to protect groups of people but only individuals, and since no individuals were mentioned in the article, there was no legal basis for upholding the complaint (Byrne 2003).

On the other hand, although information about the codes under which broadcasters and the press are supposed to operate is available to the public, it is not widely available and easily accessible – for example, in schools or accompanying the purchase of a newspaper or TV set. To be informed about the way that the media are expected to conduct themselves presupposes an active public that will *look for* this kind of information. The search for information is, however, a very time-consuming task and most people are too busy with their day-to-day responsibilities, such as work or family, and have little leisure time to devote to searching through the codes of conduct of five different overseeing bodies. The fact that some of the responsibilities of these regulating bodies overlap only makes things more confusing.

A further point is that some issues are more easily identifiable than others. It is perhaps easier to identify a breach of conduct over a programme that broadcasts explicit sexual acts than it is to identify whether a news report is false or inaccurate. To do that, one would need to be in a position that would allow some degree of authority (through first-hand experience, as a witness or someone who is directly affected), professional specialism (such as an attorney), and time to conduct research into primary sources and, of course, to gain access to such sources or alternative information sources. It is difficult to make a complaint about the lack of information on specific issues if the public is not aware of the existence of these issues in the first place.

Another restriction on citizens' ability to take formal action is the very fact that complaints can only be valid if they fall within the broader context of the guidelines as prescribed by the codes formulated by the authorities. This means that not all forms of complaints or objections have a sense of legitimacy in this process. Although this might be necessary for better control over the procedure, it does mean, however, that other forms of opinion are automatically excluded. Table 5.1 shows that there are no formal systems for appeal against the decision of a regulatory authority and no likelihood of compensation for the public. If a citizen were to be compensated s/he would have to sue the media company. Again, an appeal presupposes that the regulatory body has upheld the complaint and proceeded into the clarification of the matter addressed. However, the procedures under which an authority decides to uphold a complaint (or not) are not always transparent. Currently over 7500 complaints reach the offices of the ITC, BSC, Radio Authority and PCC combined every year, of which only a small proportion are upheld. A significant number of complaints about the print press are resolved with the editor concerned, while there is little information about the fate of complaints sent to the BSC or the ITC. Finally, involvement of the public in the process of media production takes place only after the products have been completed and disseminated – that is, after they have reached the masses. The role of the

Table 5.1: Comparative view of complaints to media regulators

	PCC	ITC	BSC	Radio Authority	BBC
Method of funding	Press industry	Licence fees paid by broadcasting companies	Public funding	Fees paid by radio industry	Licence fee until 2002
Appointment of board	Chair appointed by industry; members by Appointment Commission (also controlled by the industry)	By the Secretary of State for Culture, Media and Sport	By the Secretary of State for Culture, Media and Sport	By the Secretary of State for Culture, Media and Sport	By the Queen in Council
Code	Industry code of practice	Programme code	Codes of practice and guidance to broadcasters	Codes about programme, advertising, sponsorship, engineering	**Producers' Guidelines** most comprehensive code
Complaints issues	Articles in local, regional, national press	Strong language, sex and violence, issues of privacy and impartiality; advertising, sponsorship	Invasion of privacy and unfairness	Material that is unfair, inaccurate or likely to cause widespread offence	37 sections covering areas from impartiality to conflicts of interest, charity appeals
Time for complaint submission	Within one month of publication or the last letter received from editor	Within two months of viewing broadcast (must have seen broadcast not heard of it)	Within two months of a TV broadcast; three weeks of a radio broadcast	Broadcasters obliged to keep recordings for 42 days	–
Right to appeal	No formal appeals system	n/a	No formal appeals system	n/a	–
Percentage of cases upheld	(1998) 45 complaints upheld	Does not publish figures of complaints upheld	(1998) 3559 complaints	(1995) 89 out of 689 (447 complaints about	–

Table 5.1 continued

	PCC	ITC	BSC	Radio Authority	BBC
	out of 954 = 4.5 per cent; 58 per cent resolved with editor	(1998) 3257 complaints against commercial TV		programme) = 12.9 per cent	
Compensation for the public	None	None	None	None	–
Consequences for the media	The publication is under moral obligation to publish the PCC ruling	Broadcaster may be asked to publish apology on-screen – corrections; in extreme cases may be warned, fined or lose licence	Broadcasters or press required to publish BSC's decision	Station may be requested to broadcast an apology; serious offences may result in fine, reduction or withdrawal of licences	–

Source: adapted from PressWise; Frost 2000; Guardian Online; ITC, BSC, BBC, PCC and Radio Authority websites public is primarily one of reaction to products already in the public domain, which means that the proactive role of the public is, in this sense, seriously compromised.

In defence of personal honour: the right of reply

The role of private individuals in relation to publicized material (as expressed through complaints) notwithstanding, another aspect of the role of the public in 'answering back' to the media is of interest here. The 'right of reply' is not the same as making a complaint. A complaint may result in a correction or an apology to the person affected by the media's misconduct or mistake. The right of reply involves the right to answer back, and be given the time and opportunity not only to make corrections but even to reply to criticism and offer a personal opinion. The right of reply is one of the few instruments that can help redress the imbalance of power between the media and the public, and as such one would expect that the law would protect it. Bearing in mind the unequal access to the media, it is important that laws should seek proactively to protect the right of the freedom of expression of citizens, as this is not an exclusive right under the freedom of the press.

The right of reply is incorporated as a general principle in the Television Without Frontiers (TVWF) Directive (Article 23), but the directive is not explicit about the measures that need to be taken to provide for the right to reply:

> Without prejudice to other provisions adopted by the Member States under civil, or criminal law, any natural or legal person, regardless of nationality, whose legitimate interests, in particular reputation and good name, have been damaged by an assertion of incorrect facts in a television programme must have a right of reply or equivalent remedies. Member States shall ensure that the actual exercise of the right of reply or equivalent remedies is not hindered by the imposition of unreasonable terms or conditions. The reply shall be transmitted within a reasonable time subsequent to the request being substantiated and at a time and in a manner appropriate to the broadcast to which request refers.
>
> (TVWF Directive: Article 23)

European countries have adopted a statutory right of reply. In France, the right of reply (*droit de reponse*) gives an individual the right to respond where s/he is named in a newspaper or daily written periodical. In Germany, the right of reply means that anyone affected by a publication can respond to it within three months of the time of publishing. The individual's response must then be publicized so as to reach the same audience, and with the same forcefulness as the original material (see Communications Law Centre 1997). Switzerland is even more rigorous: the right of reply is protected to the extent that a publication can be restrained from publishing if it fails to comply. This law has been applied in at least one case (Danziger 1986; Communications Law Centre 1997). In Norway, the enforcement of the right of reply is a matter of criminal law, with severe consequences for media that do not comply with it (Humphreys 1996: 59).

Table 5.2: Legal provision for the right of reply in Europe

Country	Right of reply
Austria	Yes
France	Yes
Germany	Yes
Netherlands	Yes
Norway	Yes
Spain	Yes
Sweden	No
UK	No

Source: after Humphreys 1996; Article 19

The right of reply is particularly important today with the escalation of the gutter press and 'trash TV', as well as the sensationalism and commercialization of news. In terms of marketing, people's reputations are under constant threat of defamation and inaccuracy in the race to write headlines that will sell papers. Moreover, the development of technological means that facilitate the manipulation of images and other visual material to reinforce a story, and the fact that individuals have little access to the means of making their own stories and reaching the same audiences reached by mainstream media, highlights the necessity for statutory provision to protect a person's honour and image. The right of reply is currently in Clause 2 of the PCC Code of Practice, which states that 'a fair opportunity to reply to inaccuracies must be given to individuals or organizations when reasonably called for'. However, the efficiency of self-regulation is a questionable matter and although it is crucial to have a free press, it is also vital for a democratic society that citizens' right of expression is not compromised in the face of the rights of industry. As Table 5.1 shows, it is arguable whether the PCC or BSC have any real teeth. The former is effectively controlled by the industry and the only power the latter has is to expect the publication of its ruling by the media involved. As is the case in other European countries (Table 5.2), a person should have the right to reply to an accusation or simple reference to their name in the same format as the original publication. For example, an apology at the bottom of an inner page of a newspaper does not necessarily constitute fairness if the original story ran on the front page.

The public interest

The USA has a long history of commercial media organizations and, to a certain extent, can provide examples of the experience of a society that has prioritized commercial media over public service media. Taking into account the 'American experience' may be useful in understanding the future of the present media system in Britain. Of particular importance here is the relationship and interests of the public compared with the interests of the forces in control of contemporary communication means. Liebling, a journalist and a writer, said that in America there is freedom of the press for the person who owns one (quoted in Turow 1992: 136). This remark addresses a few important issues. First of all, it identifies the (problematic) relation of media ownership and freedom of expression. Second, it suggests that the press cannot be free for those without ownership – therefore for those without access to it. The concentration of media ownership in the hands of a few corporations with global reach and activity certainly does not contribute to free press and expression. Consequently, the concentration of the control of communication media excludes de facto the people at whom media products are directed. This exclusion can be seen as an attack on the right of expression of the citizens, consumers of media products and audiences of media messages. In the USA, as the history of media legislation shows, attempts to provide citizens with greater access to the media have seen a considerable decline. In the 1970s, broadcast media were obliged to air certain programmes under the citizen–licensee pact, a 'light' version of the public service obligation, which provided for the inclusion of specific programming (Turow 1992: 139). The broadcasters were required to fulfil their obligation in serving the community through programming that expressed citizens' interests and concerns. Failure to comply effectively meant a breach of contract and the consequence was that stations would have a very difficult case in trying to renew their licence. Conservative governments in the 1980s and pressure from the industry made this 'pact' utterly irrelevant. So the media industry was not under any obligation to deliver specific programming as required by its informative role in the community.

The dominant ideologies of media regulation in the USA claim that such intervention goes against the public good. The best way to serve the public interest is argued to be the market mechanism. These positions were strongly reinforced in the 1980s and 1990s in American communications policy as expressed through its main regulatory body, the Federal Communications Commission (FCC). As Shaw argues (1999: 169), whatever is profitable in the marketplace is considered to be the public interest. Here the public interest is used as a synonym for 'popular' or for 'what interests the public'. We have already discussed the difficulties inherent in defining the 'public' and the problems that surround the assumption that the public is a homogeneous, coherent and predictable unit. Mainly for rhetorical purposes, policy documents make frequent use of this concept. In some cases, the 'public interest' may be the ultimate aim of the state or a policy initiative, but how the concept is defined is often a matter of who has the power to make such definitions. Quite different is the understanding of the public interest by the British regulator, who interprets it as the protection of the public from harm or offence, and from the anti-competitiveness of the industry (Shaw 1999: 170).

The concept of public interest is mainly understood with reference to the 'popular', according to which commercial media adjust to changes and defend the operation of media businesses. On the other hand, public interest is also seen as a concept against a single set of values and a single ideology that would be applied to inform several aspects of the media, from structure to content. The former description of the public interest is what Held called the 'majoritarian' view and the latter is the 'absolutist' view (Held 1970; McQuail 2000: 142).

Both descriptions are equally absolutist, however, in their own capacity to follow dualism of either/or. Due to their power and special place in society, the media are unlike other businesses. Accountability, diversity and accessibility are characteristics that gain particular importance in defining the public interest. These are also the concepts that policy is based on to provide for the freedom of the press. These three values are those that characterize democratic political systems, because they guarantee the legitimacy of the political system itself. Accountability refers to the output of media workers but also the media industry itself, the process and structures that make visible and transparent the conditions and values under which media goods are created. Diversity describes the final output in the form of news programmes or entertainment, or even categorization of sources during a search on a web engine. Moreover, it refers to the backgrounds and beliefs of the people who make the input to the production of meanings. Journalists, producers, writers and directors are some of the positions held in the media industry and these should be able to reflect diversity in society. Finally, accessibility refers to the right, as well as the practical aspect for the realization of this right, of the public (in whichever form, location or condition) to access media messages, in any form, style and context these may be communicated. Access, however, also refers to the availability of the means of production of cultural goods, whether texts or artefacts, to the public, and the availability of means of transmission. The latter is probably the most important aspect about communication over the Internet, and has led many theorists and activists to place their hope for truly democratic and emancipatory communications in this new medium.

The public interest is often understood as the benefit of the whole as opposed to the benefit of the few, the elites or individuals. It is interesting that, often, a course of action is taken 'in the name of the public good' by controlling elites whose motives are questionable. Examples of these are the wars that governments engage in (for the good of the nation) or business takeovers and corporate monopolies (for the survival of free media and therefore freedom of expression). In these cases, it is not the public(s), but others on its behalf, who decide on the definition of the public interest. Here, feminist theory can help us strive for a more inclusive and egalitarian understanding of the public interest.

A strand of feminist theory (such as the work of Radway), even though from quite a different angle, has emphasized the importance of recognizing the fact that people, and therefore members of the public, occupy different and multiple positions in the hierarchy of power relations and that our knowledges and understandings reflect these positions. Caring for these knowledges and acknowledging experiences, without losing sight of the structural determinants within which such experiences and positions are produced and occupied, would lead to the expression of the public interest. Here the concept should be understood as a vital component of democratic participatory politics but also as a non-static but ever evolving concept. Precisely because it is about people, their relationships and lives within human societies (and even the relationship of human societies with the natural world), public interest cannot be a fixed and unequivocal term. Again, this should not underestimate power relations but, on the contrary, should seek to counter-balance inequalities and disadvantages.

Conclusions

The relationship between the public and the British media is multifaceted and complex. As we have seen, the public performs the role of consumer and audience. Often these roles are treated, falsely, as synonymous. The role of the public as citizen is one of the most important ones for democratic societies. The degree of involvement of the public in decision-making regarding the media differs in the form such involvement takes. Theoretically, the public enjoys rights that allow the expression of dissatisfaction with content or professional ethics. Also the public as consumer has the power to direct the development of certain products by withdrawing consumption of a specific medium. Furthermore, the public seems to be in a position to produce content and interact with the media, especially in the case of the Internet. However, all these different avenues leave only a marginal space in which the public can have significant influence on the media. The following chapter discusses the efforts of the organized public to locate, create and produce media as a way of expression and in order to counter-balance inequalities in access, ownership and control over the media.

FURTHER READING

Coleman, S. (2002) BBC Radio Ulster's *Talkback* Phone-in: Public Feedback in a Divided Public Space. In Jankowski, N. W. with Prehn, O. (eds), *Community Media in the Information Age: Perspectives and Prospects*, Cresskill, NJ: Hampton Press.
This text examines the *Talkback* programme broadcast by BBC Radio Ulster during negotiations of the Good Friday peace agreement. Attention is given to the role that citizens assume and to whom they address their opinions (mostly the political leaders, the presenter or those whose opinions they share) during the programme. The author argues that this particular case is one of the few examples where the radio becomes a free public sphere and where citizen/audience participation becomes so important in conflict/war negotiations.

Dahlgren, P. (1995) *Television and the Public Sphere*, London: Sage: Chapter 6.
This chapter brings together questions about the complexity and significance of media audiences as political actors, and seeks to identify the ways in which citizenship and the social world interact with the world of communications. Of central importance here is the concept of the public sphere, which lends itself to the analysis of institutionalized aspects of individuals and societies.

chapter six

The 'Others' of the British media

The previous chapter looked at some of the roles of the public in relation to the media. As we have seen, the fora through which citizens can intervene in the content or organization of the mainstream media are very limited. Media – and in particular 'conventional' media such as the press, radio and television – are generally run and owned by authorities or private persons. The organization of the media is also strictly hierarchical, with clear divisions between departments and management. Media operate in a similar organizational way to industries, following a specific system to obtain financial support (in the case of public service media) and are profit-orientated (commercial media). Furthermore, it is apparent that the news values of the mainstream media are not particularly receptive to stories from 'ordinary' people. Rather, the news and features that appear in the media, whether press, television or radio, are selected by professional people, who make decisions about the content that will be consumed by hundreds or thousands of people. The news or stories reported are, therefore, handled by media professionals and not by the people directly affected by or involved in the story. Compromised in their role as the 'fourth estate' – called upon to exercise criticism of economic and political powers – the mainstream media are not particularly democratic either. Other forms of media, therefore, need to fill a vast chasm in terms of the content and type of coverage of public life. This chapter, therefore, discusses the organization, production and role of non-mainstream media.

Defining the 'Others' of the media sphere

What are the alternative media? Although this may at first seem a straightforward question to answer, it is not. It is perhaps easier to understand what the alternative media are *not*. In any case, it is not easy to define them. This is probably because of their variety of forms, content, target audiences and politics, which represent a diverse, yet in many ways coherent, engagement with social, cultural and political life. First of all, the alternative media are exactly that: alternative. The term indicates a need for the 'Other', something that is not the norm. 'Alternative' means 'other than the dominant', 'other than the one under investigation'. 'Mainstream', on the other hand, indicates that which is in accordance with the normal, the standard.

The need for alternative media is neither new nor temporary. History shows that media other than those that represent dominant ideas have played an important role in the mobilization of the masses, socialization and organization of citizens, and the creation of alternative public spheres, the realm where criticism of dominant ideas is encouraged in a public and egalitarian way. This need for 'other' media has led to the creation of a diversity of media contexts and forms, which aim to counter-balance the dominance of media that are under the control of the state or other forces/authorities, and transfer control to the public.

Various definitions have tried to capture the significance and role of alternative media, often departing from accepted notions of what mainstream media are. For example, the Royal Commission on the Press (1977) provides a definition of alternative media in relation to 'standard' media. It defines the opinions represented and also the content of alternative media as 'hostile to widely held beliefs'. Furthermore, these opinions are, according to the commission, those of 'small minorities' (quoted in Atton 1999). Other definitions provide a description of characteristics. Alternative media are said to have one or more of the following characteristics:

(a) they are non profit and non commercial
(b) they are open and inclusive to the public
(c) they are more interested in social action rather than opinions
(d) they actively advocate social change
(e) they cover material that is either neglected by mainstream media or [that] is only one sided.

(Atton 1999; 2003)

John Downing (2001) argues that alternative media break somebody's rules (mainly the rules governing mainstream, standard media), although they do not break them all at the same time. For Sreberny-Mohammadi and Mohammadi (1994) alternative media are community-controlled media that produce politically sensitive and progressive messages, and are positioned as converse to major states/authorities. For Ramona Rush (1999: 81), the alternative or 'other' media 'carry news and opinions about the human condition not often seen in depth in mainstream (malestream) media'. For some scholars 'alternative' is a synonym for 'democratic'. Ó Siochrú (1999: 139) discusses the growth of democratic media around the world that are 'alternative, usually community-based . . . motivated not by profit but by solidarity, the struggle for survival or creative expression; media that empower not pacify, that create not simply repeat'. Others, like Galtung and Vincent (1992), are even more inclusive in their definition of alternative media, and expand it to define forms of journalism and content that are alternative. This includes peace journalism, and environmental or ecological journalism; this does not refer simply to the topics covered (i.e. ecological or environmental issues) but also to the politics of reporting such issues. Empowering journalism is, for these scholars, possible within commercial media but it must prioritize education, process, context and advocacy above 'objectivity'. In other words, the content of the news needs to change according to an alternative set of news values. Rush (1999) and Gallagher (1984) refer to the 'alternative' media as 'parallel' media. This is because, often, the term 'alternative' means 'second choice' and is associated with the paradigm of second-class citizens. As the authors argue, alternative media operate alongside mainstream media, but they almost never intersect.

As we can see, a shared argument is that the mainstream media's conventions do not serve the interests and well-being of ordinary people. These conventions refer to the organization of mainstream media, which is susceptible to control and/or is profit-orientated. Furthermore, the *structural* inequalities within media organizations, imbalances of gender and race, do not allow fair representation of the affairs that matter to people. Moreover, the very domination of the media by professionals – that is, specialists detached from the stories they report – has served to further alienate the public in the communication process.

A central problem in the organization of mainstream media is the dominant news values, which prioritize political and other elites over citizens, even when the stories are trivial and for entertainment purposes only. Journalists rely on the stories supplied by ministries, press offices and spokespersons, and rarely do they engage in a critical quest for the representation of all involved. Even more seldom do journalists actively advocate the public interest. The difficulties involved in any 'deviation' from the norm of news values and news-gathering are, in most cases, prohibitive to the exercise of critical journalism. Newspeople tend to work within groups of professionals doing the same sort of job, so their sources are more or less the same. Media professionals need to belong to these groups to be able to provide their newspaper or radio station with the necessary products (news items) daily. Furthermore, media industries cannot afford to exclude or miss out items reported on by their competitors.

All this demonstrates how problematic it is to suggest that the mainstream media are free to report on the things that really matter. Further, within the media world, not all mainstream media wield the same level of power. Some have privileged access to 'power centres' unavailable to others, which means that the privileged few will be those defining the news.

The format and style of the news – short, entertaining (using the dramatic elements of presentation), fast paced and based on headlines/slogans – allow little space for contextualization. Here Galtung and Vincent (1992) call for journalism that focuses on processes, backgrounds and analysis, not on 'events'. The commercialization of news into digestible (and therefore saleable) 'bites' serves the economy of corporate media. Such news forms need not, and cannot, be based on investigative journalism. In this way the cost of doing background research is kept to a minimum.

A fundamental difference between mainstream and alternative media is perceived to be their purpose, their *raison d'être*. 'The elite media set a framework within which others operate,' says Chomsky (1997). These are the media that set the agenda of news, of topics to be discussed by the mass media. Such elite media include, according to Chomsky, the *New York Times* and CNN. Elite media in the UK would therefore be Reuters, the BBC and *The Times*. Mainly, these are media organizations supported by bigger corporations, which also own them. They have very close links to centres of power such as governments, international organizations and other elites. According to Chomsky (1997), 'The real mass media are basically trying to divert people.' By this he means, for example, entertainment channels, and regional and local media. According to Albert (2002), mainstream media are predominantly 'structured in accord with and to help reinforce society's defining hierarchical social relationships'.

Alternative media's primary goal, on the other hand, is to remain independent of such organizations and undermine hierarchical social relationships. In Albert's (2002) words, 'an alternative media institution sees itself as part of a project to establish new ways of organizing media and social activity and it is committed to furthering these as a whole, and not just its own preservation'.

These very interesting approaches reveal that 'alternative' media, the 'Others' of the media world, can be understood to vary in areas from their production process to their content in a way that mainstream media cannot or will not act in accordance with. This chapter will now consider a number of 'other' media, with the aim of addressing a variety of media forms that are very distinct from the dominant ones.

Issues of hierarchy and the role of the public

The organization of alternative media usually differs from that of mainstream media, in two major areas: hierarchy and the role of the public. It would be true to say that alternative media depend on the involvement of the public in all stages of production and distribution. Indeed, they encourage the public to get involved in a number of ways. Usually the only role the public plays in the mainstream press is in the limited form of 'letters to the editor' and the like, but even these are filtered systematically; often the people who write letters to a newspaper are not taken seriously by the editors (see Wahl-Jorgensen 2002). In the alternative – or as it is often called, radical – press, reporters are actively involved in the life of their communities, and in social and political action generally. These reporters provide accounts of events that do not normally get space or airtime in the mainstream media or, if they do, tend to be represented from a dominant ideological viewpoint. The 'alternative' reporter provides personal accounts and advocacy, as well as viewpoints that are ignored or unsatisfactorily covered by the mainstream media. This approach to reporting does not fit easily with the mainstream media's news value of 'objectivity'. In most cases, the activist *is* the reporter in the radical press, thus bringing immediacy to the story.

Literature and research on the alternative media show that they intentionally open up their editorial boards to ordinary citizens. Duncombe's extensive research into US 'zines' shows that the most important contribution made by zines and underground cultures is the fact that they provide a 'free space', where imagination and creativity come together with new ways of communicating and thinking. Zines make it possible for people to be able to imagine, and perhaps create, an alternative, and therefore to escape the 'tyranny of here and now' (Duncombe 1997: 195). Fountain (1988) and Nelson (1989), in their own studies of alternative and underground culture in Britain, point to the importance of 'the people' in the organization of events, such as festivals, but also in the production of media and messages. The involvement of the public in the production process and management of their own work, based on collectivity and collaboration, prevails at the ideological forefront of alternative media.

However, this form of openness and inclusion, radically distinct from the commercial media and 'straight society' should not be romanticized, as Hesmondhalgh says (2000: 115).

The process of democratization of the media is not without its problems. Some of the most important issues here have to do with everyday practicalities, such as the organization of meetings, consensus-building and other activities that are very time-consuming. Moreover, the anti-commercial character of these media is accompanied by their struggle for financial survival, and is evident from their calls for support. Despite the fact that the participation of the public leads to an active creation of meanings that are closer to people's lives, enhance their creativity and create links to the understandings of 'Others', some major questions remain. Hesmondhalgh doubts that the work of the alternative media can have any long-term mass effect, since they are mostly read only by limited audiences, while mass audiences, who are mostly familiar with commercial media, remain unaware of them. I believe, however, that perhaps we should be looking at not only the familiarity of audiences (and thus the public) with commercial media and specific forms of popular culture, but should also recognize the process of 'schooling' the public into becoming audiences for specific media cultures, and therefore consumers for specific markets and publics for specific politics.

As Duncombe (1997) argues, hegemony is not about making the public love the status quo, but rather making them accept that there is no alternative, no other way of life. Enzensberger, in his classic essay about the consciousness industry, argues that power and authority depend not only on control over capital, industries or weapons, but increasingly over the consciousness of others: the material exploitation must have immaterial protection in order to justify itself (Enzensberger [1962] 1995: 14). Enzensberger emphasizes the importance of thought and criticism that are controlled through extreme and explicit measures such as those of censorship, prohibitions and monopoly over the means of production, and extends this to indirect mechanisms of 'self-control' and economic pressure. The alternative media are, then, seen as the means that provide a forum for the expression of ideas, experiences, thoughts and criticisms that would otherwise have been censored, either through direct censorship, self-censorship (as, for example, exercised by journalists when they know what is acceptable for publication in their newspaper) or through control over the means of production of cultural meanings, which filter those considered incompatible with the motives of the medium, whether power, profits or both.

Duncombe points out that alternative media, such as zines, 'constitute an alternative ideal of how human relations, creation and consumption *could* be organized' (my italics) (1997: 196). The reality of this alternative ideal is, of course, harsh: alternative media are under constant financial pressure to survive. Editorial meetings can be long and tiresome, the process of decision-making, in order to reach decisions based on consensus, is time-consuming. Atton (2003) discusses the editing and production of two forms of alternative media: *Counter Information*, a news sheet founded in Scotland in 1984, and *Undercurrents*, a video magazine produced by activists around the world. Both media, although different in form and location (the former is a print-based production and local, while the latter is electronic and international), face enormous financial difficulties that cannot easily be overcome by self-exploited labour and/or donations, or other means of non-traditional product financing. *Counter Information* reaches a circulation of 12,000 and covers issues that are of broader importance, such as workers' issues, protests and local stories of 'wider relevance', as well as issues that are generally not covered in the mainstream media. Although the magazine is open to contributions from the community, there is a core of five to ten people who attend editorial meetings. This number, although small, is adequate for everyone to have the chance to make a substantial contribution, and helps in maintaining a team of manageable size to make decisions based on consensus. *Undercurrents* was produced by activists involved in environmental campaigns around the world (the last issue was produced in 1999) and was based in London. It was a project that combined both amateur video recording/writing and professional editing provided by Small World Media, a film production company specializing in environmental and political features. The involvement of professionals 'sympathetic' to activism was necessary due to the nature of the product. Atton (2003) argues that it is precisely this emphasis on the everyday experience of activist and producer, in different roles and situations, that encapsulates the spirit of alternative media.

Resources and the media

These examples of alternative media demonstrate the difficulty inherent in adopting production practices that democratize the processes and content involved. The difficulty is mainly a matter of resources. Money, means, time and skills are distributed unequally in the dominant economic system. The picture of the world provided by statistical data is gloomy. According to the United Nations Development Report (UNDP), 99 per cent of the world's wealth is owned by men, and one in four people on the planet lives on less than $1 a day (Gallagher 1986; Sutcliffe 2001). In Britain, men earn on average 35 per cent more than women (*Guardian Media Guide* 2002). The ratio of national income and purchasing power between the richest and poorest regions in the world has risen five times within the last 150 years: it was 3:1 in 1820 and had risen to 16:1 by 1997 (Sutcliffe 2001: Section 114).

Although in wealthy nations, such as the UK or the USA, wages would be expected to have improved, and the division between poor and rich reduced, this is not necessarily the case. In the USA, the owners and controllers of capital, such as companies, saw their income increase 11-fold between 1960 and 1999, whereas those who depend on wages saw little or no change. The data clearly show that the rich 'have gained at the expense of the poor' (see Sutcliffe 2001; EPI 1999; 2000; Global Financial Data 2000). Further, there are global patterns of wage inequality that are based on sex and race discrimination. For example, worldwide, the sexual division of labour shows major inequalities and differences in women's and men's work: women generally do more work than men, but much of this work is unpaid. They do less paid work (only one-third of women's work is paid) and are paid less for doing it than men.

These are a just few simple examples of inequalities in the distribution of wealth and resources in the world – they omit many other dimensions, such as inequality in terms of, access to education, food and cultural development. What these examples demonstrate, however, is the importance of resources to human development. According to the United Nations, human development is measured by a wide range of economic and social 'life indicators', which include cultural development (literacy and education), income, diet and life expectancy. The importance of understanding human development lies in its relationship, among other things, to full social and political participation in society. The notion of human development may also help us to understand why it is so difficult to find resources and sustain them for projects and activities that do not merely serve to pursue financial profit for companies or nations.

These examples should also help us to understand the mission, motivation and background of alternative media (as well as their content), and the ways of expressing and producing meanings that communicate those motives. As Traber (1985) points out, alternative media bring in 'alternative social actors'. These are the people who are directly affected by social and economic inequalities and are normally excluded from the official channels of public communication, 'the poor, the oppressed, the marginalized' or, in the words of Rush (1999: 75), the 'minoritized majority'. Lack of resources is the most serious obstacle to the maintenance of such projects. The financial survival of alternative media depends mainly on donations from people who are among the lowest paid, volunteers who are prepared to work for no pay, and in some cases subscriptions. Advertising revenues are minimal or totally absent, since alternative media tend to be very selective (they will only accept advertisements for environmentally friendly products, for example). Many alternative media simply refuse to accept advertisements at all, so that they can preserve their editorial independence (often at the expense of their financial survival).

However, the mechanisms of the material production of the media (such as printing a newspaper, for example) and their distribution are far from straightforward either. Distribution networks often refuse to offer their services unless the media involved are capable of generating a profit. This helps to explain why some of these alternative media do not expand nationally. It is also important to recognize, however, that in some cases, the producers of alternative media are not at all interested in using 'mainstream' methods of dissemination. Atton (1999) offers examples of alternative media that rely partly or wholly on reproduction and redistribution by 'consumers' through photocopying and further circulation of material, therefore openly promoting anti-copyright tactics. Such UK-based publications are the print zines *Squall* (whose content is devoted to the homeless, travellers and squatters) and *Do or Die* (related to the radical organization Earth First!). It appears that those media organizations that are run by a small, dedicated core group of editors have the best chances of survival. One such example is the *Big Issue*, sold by the homeless and dealing with issues such as life on the street. As Atton (1999) rightly points out, however, although the cause is noble (part of the sales price goes to the individual selling the paper), the content is totally controlled by professional journalists and the whole project was subsidized by businesses such as the Body Shop. Here Atton differentiates between the *advocacy* press and the *grassroots* press. The latter is seen as more open to the interventions of the public and is therefore more democratic.

Women's alternative media

Advocacy and grassroots media may be different in their organizational structures, but this does not exclude them from fulfilling a role of giving voice to 'alternative social actors'. However, even alternative media – the main forum via which the voices of the 'oppressed' can be heard – have maintained attitudes that exclude others: sexism has not been uncommon in magazines of the underground. In their historical account of British alternative culture in the

1960s and 1970s, two studies record the treatment of women both within the organizational structures of the magazines and also in terms of women's representation in their content. Fountain (1988: 101) describes the resignation of female secretary Anne Scott (one of only two female workers on the magazine – there was another in the editorial department) from the underground magazine the *Dwarf*. Her resignation letter suggested that her comrades should imagine what it is to be 'black, not white' and to 'have cunts, not cocks'. Sheila Rowbotham (the other female member of staff at the *Dwarf*) also left. The women's movement had begun and bypassed male radical politics. Numerous conferences, meetings and feminist media have led to the strengthening of the 'second wave' of the feminist movement, which drew upon the work of Simone de Beauvoir, Betty Friedan, Germaine Greer and Marxist-orientated work coming from Germany and the USA (Fountain 1988). The alternative press of the times, with magazines such as *IT*, *Oz* and *Dwarf* remained sexist and ignorant of women's issues. Nelson (1989) argues that the British counter-culture and its media were really men's counter-culture and men's media.

Spare Rib was born in 1972, signalling the birth of the 'daughter of the underground press', according to its founding editor (Nelson 1989: 140). The feminist press came to serve not only as the voice of the oppressed, but also as an alternative to male-dominated alternative politics. The 'mainstream' underground, via its press, never really adequately or seriously dealt with women's politics; it did not even consider women as allies (Nelson 1989: 140). The women's liberation movement gave life to and was given voice by a wide range of means of expression, not just in Britain but around the world. The *Women's Newsletter* (UK), *New Directions for Women* (USA), *Rat* (USA) and *Emma* (Germany) were just some of the alternative media born to express cultural and political resistance. Most of them ceased to exist, but others continued into the 1990s. *Emma*, the German feminist magazine, celebrated its 25th birthday in 2002, with 60,000 copies sold per issue. Established in 1977, *Emma* sold 200,000 copies of its inaugural issue and a further 100,000 reprints. A marketing survey shows that 78 per cent of Germans know what *Emma* is, and the name of its founding editor, Alice Schwarzer; 76 per cent of Germans believe that *Emma* represents the interests of women (von Glinski 2002). The readers of the magazine are women aged between 20 and 39 years old.

One of the major contributions of the feminist press and movement of the 1970s was that issues central to women's lives were given some visibility; some have even been integrated, to a degree, into mainstream magazines. We need to be careful, though, not to assume that discussing issues of career or contraception in mainstream magazines such as *Cosmopolitan* is a sign of the 'completion' of women's liberation. Commercial media, and the cultural industries in general, tend to accommodate social change and incorporate some of its elements into their mechanisms for profit-making. The transformation of ideas and social demands into trends that will generate a profit is a strategy that does not allow the challenges of the original ideas to be a threat to the system that supports their commercialism. So when *Cosmopolitan* offers advice on professional development, it does so without challenging the existing work regime, such as long hours, lack of provision for parents, pensions or even inequality in pay, and without proposing an alternative model. Similarly, *Cosmopolitan* and other magazines have editorial pages devoted to eating disorders (exacerbated by the commodification of the female body through the marketization of slim bodies, and surgically altered and mutilated body parts, such as breast enlargements and reductions) next to pages advertising 'lite' foods and drinks, or an ideal female appearance achieved through the purchase of cosmetics. This does not necessarily serve their readers well. Instead, they serve their advertisers, who need readers to form their audiences. In their turn, the mainstream media have to appear to respond to social demands for change (recognition and promotion of women's independence and equal rights, for example).

The British *Spare Rib: A Women's Liberation Magazine* explored what it meant to be a woman in patriarchal and counter-culture by giving voice to issues central to women's lives, such as the obvious contradictions between femininity and feminism, pleasure and ideology, independence, capitalism and women's liberation. The magazine had written one of the most successful *her*stories for 20 years, until its last issue (it ran from 1972 to 1993). The opportunity to 'tell your own story' is the driving force behind the foundation of much women's media. The New York punk rock zine *Riot Grrrl* emphasizes that its politics is the politics of subjectivity and contributors' individual politics. Personal expression is the cornerstone of this magazine, which encompasses third-wave feminism and cultural expression, but it is not an end in it itself (Duncombe 1997: 68). Riot grrrls form a community and see themselves as a political force, an empowering one with the function to raise consciousness and construct a new model of community. Duncombe (1997) points to the question of how to make it possible to turn the politics of personal and cultural expression – that is, the revolution that takes place 'right here in these pages' of *Riot Grrrl* – into action that will change the system.

A great number of women's media are not always directly produced by grassroots groups, but their content depends on information, networking and stories provided by those at grassroots level (i.e. directly from the public) which then find their way into the public sphere with the help of professionals. International alternative media and communication networks also depend on the collaboration between the ordinary public and media professionals. Such an international and alternative information source is the *Women's International Network (WIN) News*, which was founded in 1975 by journalist and academic Fran P. Hosken to 'enable women to communicate about their own concerns and issues regardless of political barriers and manipulation by mainstream media' (Hosken 1996: 211). *WIN News* provides information about projects and programmes around the world, thus facilitating contacts and networking among women activists and providing a female perspective on international decisions (Hosken 1996). It had been financed by subscriptions for many years until it was accepted by major libraries. Its topics have included reports on female genital mutilation, violence against women worldwide and human rights, as well as studies and reports that could not find a home in the mainstream publishing houses. *WIN News* has been running for more than two decades. WINGS (Women's International News Gathering Service), a feminist radio service that provides programmes around the world, has also survived successfully since the early 1980s, but not without its founders and members going through periods of extreme financial difficulties, with homelessness not being unusual (Werden 1996). WINGS airs on many radios, and in community and women's media around the world. It deals with women's issues – that doesn't mean another 'new American diet', but stories that fail even to catch the attention of the mainstream media. One such story was that of the Swedish women MPs' coalition to introduce legislation to allow the prosecution of the patrons of prostitution in the early 1990s, which successfully extended to the protection of 'sex workers' in the late 1990s.

The brave new world

At the dawn of the new millennium, the alternative press, and indeed many dimensions of the alternative press, have begun to utilize two crucial tools for the project of resistance: the building of supportive networks and the use of the Internet. Alternative expression has always used technologies and networking, building alliances, but the instant and trans-spatial nature of the Internet makes the establishing of contacts and the creation of electronic fora and zines easier, more immediate and faster. All this, of course, is only achievable if access to the Internet and some web-design skills are available.

A recent example of the ability of new technologies to bring together dispersed, small, local or new publications is that of the Independent News Collective (INK), which acts as a distributor of the alternative press. Other examples include the *Zmag*'s portal to independent media around the world. However, zines and other media, such as video, have also gone on-line to increase their visibility and to facilitate interaction with their publics. The *f-word young UK feminism* on-line zine is one such new publication; it is a feminist zine for 'young women' that is itself very young. It was launched in March 2001 because, as its founder says, 'it's the sort of thing I would like to read, but didn't seem to exist'. The zine addresses issues that never seem to go out of date, such as discrimination and body image, but also deals with the tensions and complementarities of 'older' and third-wave feminists, an aspect of which can be found in the debate as to whether the magazine should remain open to 'young' UK feminists only or should include 'older' feminists too. The zine also gathers criticism of mainstream publications and media (the TV programme *Ally McBeal* and *Cosmopolitan* magazine are two that are currently in the spotlight). What is especially interesting is the use of language and sources common to zines abroad and in the UK. For example, the founder refers to 'grrrls' and media like *Bitch*, *Ms* (America's leading feminist magazine) and even *Spare Rib*. The tradition of radical, independent expression is, then, evolving alongside the social realities that created it, and sometimes transcending them.

FURTHER READING

Atton, C. (2002) *Alternative Media*, London: Sage.
This book discusses the alternative media system(s) in the UK and the USA. It pays particular attention to the economics and production organization of alternative media, and is a very useful and accessible book. The author addresses the close links between alternative media and social movements, and the active involvement of readers in the production of media output.

Cottle, S. (2000) A Rock and a Hard Place: Making Ethnic Minority Television. In Cottle, S. (ed.), *Ethnic Minorities and the Media*, Buckingham/Philadelphia: Open University Press. Although not directly addressing the issue of alternative media, the chapter deals with programming that is not often regarded as part of 'mainstream' output. In particular, the author discusses the difficulties in overcoming BBC bureaucracy, but also looks at economic and market-related problems in the production and distribution of material that seeks to appeal not only to audiences of ethnic minorities in Britain but also to wider audiences.

Pimlott, H. R. (2000) Mainstreaming the Margins. The Transformation of *Marxism Today*. In Curran, J. (ed.), *Media Organisations in Society*, London: Arnold.
The author examines the case of *Marxism Today* as an alternative publication that gained national exposure. His argument is that, despite the fact that the journal had access to the structures that helped it survive economically, this was not the only reason behind its achievement of a national presence. The journal was reported on by mainstream media that were seeking to advance a different agenda.

Rowe, M. (ed.) (1982) *Spare Rib Reader. 100 Issues of Women's Liberation*, Harmondsworth: Penguin Books.
A classic book, with a selection of *Spare Rib* writings from the most intensive period of the women's liberation movement in the UK. A wealth of articles and short features provides a valuable overview of the issues addressed by the magazine. These are organized into themes such as violence, image, the Arts, work and health, among others. The book's Introduction offers an insider's view of the conceptualization and production of *Spare Rib* as an underground medium that went on to become a legend.

chapter seven

Moments and contexts in the British media

The following case studies represent three classic examples of the British media. They are different to each other, but all three constitute moments and contexts we encounter in some way in our consumption experience: *Injustice*, an alternative – but for its directors a mainstream – film, which has known international recognition; the case of the UK pornography industry as a sub-industry on its way to the mainstream; and the BBC as the apotheosis of public service broadcasting and therefore representative of the media 'establishment'. These topics have been selected because they bring together a number of issues discussed in this book. These cases address the issue of 'public interest', and the dynamics of ownership and production (Chapter 2). They also discuss policy implications (Chapters 3 and 4) in relation to the public interest (see Chapter 5).

Injustice: an alternative mainstream film?

Injustice is a film made by the collective Migrant Media, a documentary production company set up in the 1980s with the aim of producing material about immigration and race that would be shown by mainstream channels. In 1995 Migrant Media made a film (*Justice Denied*) about the death of Joy Gardner, who suffocated during a deportation raid; the film was shown by Channel 4. At around the same time, Ken Fero and Tariq Mehmood started the filming of *Injustice*. It would take seven years to complete.

The film explores cases of violent death in police custody in Britain and is, as *Time Out* (2001) argues, 'the most politically provocative British film of recent years'. Since 1969, 1000 people have died while in police custody, most of them black. The film addresses the fact that these deaths have never been taken to trial, even when 'unlawful killing' has been established. The film follows the stories of the families of the victims in their campaign to bring those responsible to justice.

The case of *Injustice* as a media product is interesting for a number of reasons. The production process of the film makes it alternative in many ways. The exceptionally long time it took to make the documentary, renders it unprofitable in the sphere of market-driven, fast-paced television. The directors found it difficult to get any substantial financial support, since none of the major broadcasters was willing to commission the work, fearing a negative response from the police. In some cases, although the broadcasters showed an interest in the project, they proposed that a police officer be interviewed (Red Pepper 2001). For the directors, the documentary's role was to correct an injustice and let the voices of the victims' families be heard. The directors took a direct ideological and moral position, which went against the mainstream claims of 'objectivity' and impartiality. Such 'objectivity' would demand the representation of both sides in the film. However, the fact that these cases of death in custody have remained undealt with, and many people have effectively been silenced, prompted the film-makers to voice a particular perspective.

The documentary was financed by the team involved, reaching costs of £400,000. Only one-tenth of this total cost was recouped (Fero 2002: interview); the remainder has been paid over time by the creators themselves. The problems continued after the completion of the film, as none of the major broadcasters was willing to broadcast it – not even Channel 4, a broadcaster associated with alternative and progressive programming. When screenings of *Injustice* were arranged in several venues, the British Police Federation issued warnings that movie theatre owners might be liable to charges of libel if the film were to be found defamatory. These warnings created a chilly climate and theatre owners decided not to permit screenings in their theatres. The result was effective censorship of the film. Public support was beginning to grow, however, deriving from the social networks of relatives and families of victims, their supporters and empathetic citizens. So the screenings took place in 'alternative' venues: a tactic of 'guerrilla' screenings was employed, which slowly led to the Police Federation ceasing its warnings. In the meantime, the film had been shown at several festivals and conferences and at movie theatres around the world. It has become a work around which a social movement is being built.

The directors deny that this is an alternative film. Ken Fero says that he wanted to make a mainstream film that would be shown widely (interview with the author, 6 February 2002). The conditions of the production of the film, however, distinguish it from mainstream media. It was made through the collaboration of the film-makers with the people directly affected by its subject. As discussed in Chapter 6, one of the major differences between mainstream and alternative media is that the latter is based on the participation of the public, the 'grassroots', in the production process. The making of the film brought different people together to work towards a common goal, but the impact of the product itself also grew alongside the organization of this group (United Friends and Family Campaign). Advocacy (the act of representing the interests of vulnerable groups) and activism (the active campaigning of citizens for social matters) are inseparable elements in grassroots works. They constitute an integrated 'set' of factors, aim and content – that is, the public–product–effect. The fact that the work derives its themes and resources from a grassroots level allows it to produce content that deals with, and calls for, activism.

The usual difficulties, for alternative media, of finance and dissemination are also present in this particular case and give rise to two main observations. On the one hand, the production and distribution of a factual feature-length programme depend a great deal on the availability of resources. As a product on the margins of the broadcasting and film industry – not only in terms of its subject matter, but also its 'reason for being' – *Injustice* is not 'consumed' in the same fashion and at the same venues as Hollywood films or *Panorama*. This case demonstrates that the spaces available to controversial material exist predominantly outside the realm of mainstream media, but nevertheless shows that non-aligned ways of production and distribution can be accepted and supported by the public.

Finally, the role of communications policy cannot be overstated. This discussion shows that, under British libel law, it is the responsibility of the media to prove that their material is not defamatory. In other European countries, if the media provide evidence that a crime has been committed, the public prosecutor has the obligation to undertake an investigation into the alleged crime. In this case, the possibility of its makers being sued by the Police Federation hindered the distribution of the film, at least initially, due to the enormous costs that would be involved in taking legal action. The effect is that individual citizens, in a consumer, business or political role, cannot afford to criticize powerful state institutions, especially those such as the police force, unless they have enormous financial resources to bear the costs of any legal action. Organization of citizens may manage to garner the necessary resources, however, these observations raise questions as to the practicality of the existing system of libel law and freedom of expression. The film also illustrates the significance of the mass media in our era, in their 'unfashionable' roles of educating and informing, and challenges British society to consider whether civil rights are effective rights if the means necessary to exercise them are not available. It also shows, however, that alternative media can be successful, despite being excluded from mainstream channels of funding and distribution.

The UK pornography industry

Pornography is seen as an industry separate from the all-too-familiar mass media. It is not part of the mainstream nor of the alternative media spheres, yet it is widespread and mainstream in its profits and distribution. Despite legislation that allegedly aims to control the content and spread of pornography, it has continued to grow, to a point that it constitutes the main route to profit for telecommunications companies.

Pornography is usually understood to be visual, audio or written material of sexual explicitness and nakedness, which aims to induce sexual arousal. Pornography is a multi-billion-pound industry that makes its money from the production and distribution of content solely based on sexual acts. Its consumption is a social practice whereby gender relations are exemplified and reinforced. The object of pornography is the female body, or the 'feminized' body of males in non-heterosexual material. Furthermore, pornography is the object of policy, usually confined in the discursive space of censorship or obscenity. The content and narratives of pornography are, effectively, specific ideologically loaded representations of sexuality, sexual relations and, ultimately, women. They contribute to the reflection and reproduction of social relationships, a system of labour relations and a context of particular meanings.

Here, pornography is discussed as a powerful economic factor in the media industry. The pornography industry uses a variety of methods to legitimize its product. At a discursive level, women are used to demonstrate their endorsement of pornography and therefore help alleviate the image of the industry as misogynistic or counter to the morals of society. Women's photographs are accompanied by statements about the entertainment or experience value of having their photographs taken for 'soft' porn magazines, such as *Playboy* or *Penthouse*, or mainstream 'lads'' magazines, such as *Loaded*, *FHM* or *For Men*, and their 'special editions', such as 'sexy' calendars or *Spunk Loving Sluts*. The women used in these magazines, and in newspapers such as the *Sun* are quoted as feeling empowered, or free and happy to show their bodies; the comments under the photographs are directed at the male reader, reinforcing the idea that the women photographed are only too happy, too eager to please. 'Sadly, fellas, Karolina is NOT included in the price' reads the caption under (the pretext of) underwear fashion photographs in the *Sun* (20 November 2003: 3).

Reality TV programmes use sex as the core item of their 'investigations' into the lives of holiday reps or young British tourists on trips to holiday destinations. Besides the ignorant and xenophobic representations of indigenous people, such programmes use images of half-nude female bodies to sensationalize their content. Since the late 1990s, a number of television programmes produced under the pretext of 'exploring' the industry's labour relations have used meta-pornography – that is, the use of pornographic material to 'discuss' pornography – to gain audiences on mainstream television. Such programmes, along with films like *Boogie Nights* and also the fashion industry (with legends such as 'porn star in training' on T-shirts), are part of a strategy of mainstreaming the most controversial, but most profitable, media industry in the world.

Pornography is visible in our everyday lives, on billboards, mobile phones advertisements, buses: everywhere human beings are reduced to body parts to sell objects through sexual connotation. Pornography, as an industry, is also very close to the politics of the UK. The Labour Party, for instance, has accepted a £100,000 donation from Richard Desmond, owner of the *Daily Express*, *OK!* magazine and a series of pornographic titles, such as *Asian Babes* and *Big Ones*, as well as the adult Fantasy Channel. Critics have pointed out how 'helpful' the close relationship between the Labour Party and Desmond has been for both sides: Desmond was not referred to the Competition Commission when he acquired the *Express* titles, while Labour continues to have two friendly newspaper titles on its side (Ahmed and Barnett 2002).

In its strategy to 'mainstream' its product, and therefore acquire mainstream advertising space and more customers, the pornography industry employs several methods to legitimize its content. Society's attitudes to sexually explicit material are changing, and it is reasonable to say that in the western world such explicitness is more widely acceptable than before. This very selective 'liberation' is more ready to accept explicit material that adheres to the heterosexual norms of sexual behaviour, while sexual relations between women in prime-time soap operas still cause fainting incidents among viewers.

In Britain, one of the strictest European countries in terms of regulating nudity in the media, the law changed in 2002 to legalize the production and purchase of hardcore pornography. Here, a useful observation should be made: hardcore pornography refers predominantly to the depiction of aroused male but *not* female genitalia. Pornography has been regulated mainly within the context of the Obscene Publications Act, which makes illegal any content that is likely to corrupt. Obscenity, and hardcore pornography, although not synonymous or necessarily related, are mostly associated with the act of male erection, an understanding that involves indirect ideological assumptions about the involuntary nature of the act of male erection. As Dworkin argues, the obscenity law has been used against writers and artists who have tried to push back the boundaries of what is socially defined as obscene (1996: 135). However, while the law recognizes the act in erection, it does not recognize the act in pornography. In other words, Dworkin argues that, in pornography, it is not the penis that is in question, although its use becomes the means of another act, which remains 'unpunished' by the law: the act of subordination. For Dworkin, social subordination of women takes place in four places: in hierarchy (and inferiority); objectification ('when a human being is made less than a human, turned into a thing or commodity . . . a person is de-personalized, so that no individuality or integrity is available socially' (Dworkin 1996: 139)); submission, which in 'a condition of inferiority and objectification is usually essential for survival' (1996: 139); and finally violence.

Although the issue of pornography is complex and multifaceted, most public debates refer to pornography in relation to freedom of expression. Arguments for the regulation of the pornography industry are countered by arguments against censorship, limiting the debate to a simple duality of pornography vs censorship. Furthermore, pornography is often debated on the grounds of nakedness, sexuality or explicitness of images. Feminist accounts of pornography (Dworkin 1981; 1996; MacKinnon 1985; Itzin 1992) have concentrated on the causal relationship between pornography consumption and real-life crimes, such as rape, or the long-term effects of prostitution, exploitation, degradation and inequality. Feminist scholarship and activism, however, do not hold naively over-simplified positions that support censorship at all costs – or even pornography at all costs. Expanding on the examination of cause-and-effect of pornography, feminists have begun to address the conditions that produce certain kinds of pornography:

> Thus, where the first trend in pornography research establishes a general framework for the analysis of pornographic production and regulation in modern societies, this line of enquiry suggests ways of conducting particular pieces of research which investigate a variety of sexually explicit texts and their contexts.
>
> (Attwood 2004)

The uses of pornography have to be placed within a wider context of gratification, physical, verbal or other abuse, and, ultimately, social relationships themselves. Is the consumption of pornography in the army or at times of war a mere 'free-time' occupation? Is the enactment of pornographic scenes simply a matter of consenting adults? What is the relationship between pornography and prostitution? Is the alleged empowerment of women as the 'protagonists' in pornographic material proven by 'high' salaries? Who owns the copyright for these works, and do these workers have any rights over their own images? What do language and the represented action *to* someone tell us about the position of the social group of women?

The policy dimensions associated with pornography refer to the public consumption of sexually explicit images. The immediate association is that of censorship, which is understood as the opposite of freedom of expression. Feminist analysis has shown that the issue of pornography should be looked at in the context of sexual inequality and power relations, where sex is the means through which subordination is enacted. Although it is beyond the scope of this book to discuss the complex issue of pornography, it is worth considering that beyond offending 'bourgeois sensibilities' or Britain's puritanism, pornography plays an important role in exemplifying and reinforcing power relations. Paying attention to the contexts, language and discourses surrounding the images of pornography, but also of written pornographic stories, is a necessary stage of the study of pornography and a central element in understanding its effects.

Currently, the pay-per-view (PPV) market in Europe is growing at breakneck speed, and projected revenues from PPV in 2006 look likely to be 11 times more than they were in 2000, reaching $4.9 billion. The paid-for content is predominantly sports, adult content and games (Datamonitor 2001). The new technologies of 3G (third-generation) phones are turning to pornography to boost market dispersion, with expected traffic of adult content reaching 80 per cent of content traffic, making $4 billion for the pornography industry (of a total $70 billion) from mobile telephony in the USA. Private Media Group (a pornography company) is working with all operators in Britain for the supply of pornography through short text messages (SMS) (PMN 2003). It is not only mobile telephone companies that are working with Private Media, however: Hot Rod Productions exclusively distributes content from the Private Media Group in Britain on DVDs, television and the Internet. Financial analysts argue that for Internet service providers (ISPs), pornography offers one of the most important sources of profit; in Great Britain a quarter of all Internet traffic is directed at porn sites (Jaques 2001). Adult magazines are one of only four magazine categories that show growth in market share, according to COMAG, the major British magazine and press distributor (COMAG 2003).

The pornography industry is not only one of the most lucrative media industries, though. Attempts in recent years to mainstream the production, distribution and therefore consumption of pornographic material reflect the strong links of the industry with mainstream media. Figure 7.1 shows a few examples of the ways in which the UK pornography industry is linked with mainstream media production and distribution. So-called 'soft porn' magazines or pseudo-intellectual 'softcore' magazines (also called, and certainly featuring under the same 'adult' category as, men's magazines) are owned by publishing houses and media companies such as the ICP, which owns 80 per cent of the UK's magazines. IPC is now owned by AOL Times Warner, which also produces cartoons and children's programmes, owns elite media such as *Time*, and owns ISPs which make access to pornographic sites available. The owners of these sites are difficult to locate, but generally in the British domain some are owned by Northern & Shell, the same company that owns *OK!* magazine, *Express* newspapers and a number of sex phone lines and the Fantasy Channel (which shows pornography and is euphemistically called an 'adult' channel). The Fantasy Channel is carried by ntl, BSkyB and Telewest, which also carry other pornographic channels, such as the Adult Channel (which ranks number two in top ten television channels in the UK). The websites of these channels further complement the television content by 'extending' it to other features, more explicit images and aggressive language, and also containing links to other sites and products.

These are just a few examples from an industry whose growth is showing no sign of ending or declining. Pornographic content is indeed becoming more mainstream: the shelves of WHSmith play host to an increasing number of blokes', or lads' mags with pornographic content, and images available on the Internet are becoming more extreme and vulgar.

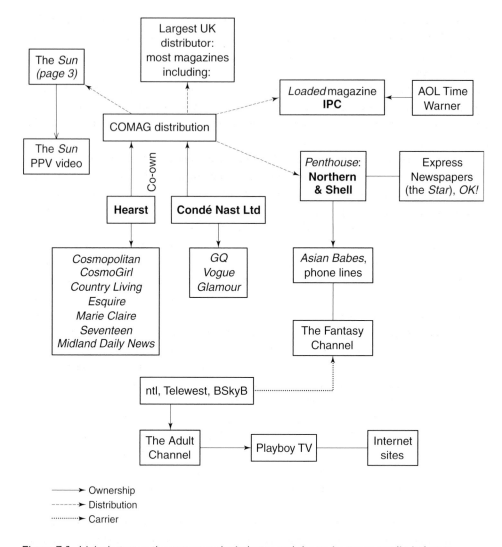

Figure 7.1 Links between the pornography industry and the mainstream media industry

The BBC and the world

Public service broadcasting: a British invention?

It is generally accepted that the birth of the BBC signalled the beginning of an era in broadcasting, based on the politics of public service and the common good. There is probably also good reason for the British to take pride in having 'invented' the model of public service broadcasting, a model that has developed substantially in Europe and come to symbolize one of Britain's, and Europe's, media trademarks. Having observed the outcome of the commercialization of broadcasting in the United States, the British government decided to take control of the development of broadcasting. In particular, the broadcasting system was regarded as holding a very special place in the cultural life of the country and the ideals associated with its *raison d'être* were those of cultural diffusion, information and education for the common good (Hutchison 1999a).

The organizational dimensions of the BBC were determined by the recommendations made by a system of semi-independent committees, appointed by subsequent governments. These committees addressed a number of issues related to the broadcasting landscape of Britain, where the BBC occupied a central position. The issue of the independence of the BBC, quality of programming, questions of funding and the mission of the institution remained central to most committee deliberations. The ideals of 'public service' maintained their momentum for several decades and characterized the mission of the system as a national institution. These ideals referred to a commitment to 'quality' programming, initially associated with the 'high arts', impartial and objective information and a mission to educate the public. Certainly, the claims over impartiality and objectivity can be contested, as perhaps can the idea that 'quality programming' is a synonym for programmes about the high arts.

The BBC owes much of its dominance as the role model of public service broadcasting in Europe to a combination of facts. First, it is of significance that Great Britain had already established a communications empire before the founding of the BBC, which allowed it access to large audiences. This same capacity allowed the BBC to continue its broadcasts at a time when the credibility of European broadcasters suffered under totalitarian regimes and wars.

At the beginning of the Second World War the BBC offered little real information in its bulletins, remaining true to the government's decision to involve as few intellectuals as possible. However, the growing dissatisfaction with the service, and its loss of credibility among the British public forced the BBC to expand, grow and involve an increasing number of intellectuals (Curran and Seaton 2003: 129). It was at the same time that the institution decided that the voices of its newsreaders should sound neutral and official – this, together with the fact that occupied Europe had access only to the BBC as an outside source of information, helped create a particular image for the institution. The BBC's World Service was staffed by refugees, who did not always agree with the institution's approach to their countries. Nevertheless, listening to BBC radio in the occupied zones was considered by many to be an act of resistance in itself (Curran and Seaton 2003). For some countries, civil war and dictatorship continued the devastating work begun by the Second World War and BBC radio, later joined by the German news agency Deutsche Welle, continued to play an important role in these countries.

The fact that the BBC had an image as one of the major 'independent' sources of information does not mean that it *was* an independent source, however. As Curran and Seaton note (2003: 145), when it came to covering issues related to the Allies, the BBC followed government policy, which in some cases paid homage to Russian comradeship (similar pictures were often available in the press and on television in the United States); these discourses would contradict Cold War propaganda discourses once the war was over. Further, the BBC's views about the war were identified with the government's, and very little representation of the public interest, such as inadequate facilities and the poor organization of air-raid shelters, was ever advocated by the institution. Under these conditions, it is questionable whether the public service broadcasting system enabled or facilitated debates that were in the public interest. In this respect, 'public ownership' structures did not prove to be better equipped to provide the kind of content and mode of address that would grant visibility to public concerns and address social issues that were in the interests of those most affected by the economic and political conditions of the country.

The BBC and the British government

The uneasy relationship between government and BBC reached an all-time low much later, during the Falklands War. As discussed in Chapter 1, the BBC was attacked by then Prime Minister Margaret Thatcher for calling the troops 'British' and not '*our* troops'. The politics of tension between government and broadcaster can be argued to derive from the anxiety of governments that uncontrolled information will reach the public. Furthermore, the media's power to support a particular political party can be very influential in the election of government. Thatcher's politics were also driven by an ideologically based distaste for all things public (publicly owned companies and institutions were sold to private owners during the reign of the Tory government). The policy of privatization continued under 'New' Labour, and goes on to this day.

It is reasonable to say, in fact, that the BBC has often been under attack from most British governments. This tension can be seen in the ways in which government tries to determine the future of the corporation. Since the intensification of liberalization of public ownership, the very mission of the BBC has been called into question, alongside the legitimacy of its funding resources. Since the late 1970s/early 1980s, the BBC has had to face a series of policies that have enabled private corporations to expand and dominate media markets; the country has even faced the 'bending' of rules to accommodate a significant merger between ITV companies Carlton and Granada in 2003.

At the same time, the BBC has often been warned by the government for not fulfilling its public service duties in its programming. The licence-fee funding method has been questioned often enough by private companies, but also in media debate, and has received precious little support from the government. At a time where corporatist interests prevail, all European public service broadcasters have the increasingly difficult task of defending their model and operation within a multi-source media system. However, the flourishing of the BBC, against all odds, means that it remains a powerful example of a successful PSB. Certainly, European PSBs do not have the same history nor means at their disposal as the BBC, but perhaps what it is most important to defend is the principle of broadcasting with a public service ethos. What this would mean for the future is not a continuation of the old model of PSBs but a public ethos of a broadcaster that stays close to the public and addresses social issues, even when these are not in favour of certain institutions.

The most persistent threat to the BBC has been the withdrawal of its funding. Several suggestions regarding the finances of the BBC have been discussed over the years, most of which seek to find sources of revenue other than the licence fee. This matter will be reviewed again in 2006, under the Communications Act, while, at the time of writing, the new super-regulator Ofcom is conducting a major investigation into the future of public service broadcasting. It is true that since the BBC is funded by television set owners (i.e. the public), its programming should adhere to areas as broad and diverse as possible. The commercial broadcasters, according to this logic (which is the market logic), do not share the same responsibility for public service programming because their services are purchased through the process of supply and demand. This is a conventional market-orientated argument. It accepts that the media are just industries. This is the reason why, in the current climate of intensified privatization and concentration of ownership, the BBC partly defies the logic of the market. It still enjoys high ratings (over 40 per cent for BBC1 and BBC2), while all five terrestrial channels together control more than 75 per cent of UK audiences (Bromley 2001).

The BBC's commercial arm, BBC Worldwide, is particularly successful: its sales of documentaries, such as *Walking with Dinosaurs*, and game shows, such as *The Weakest Link*, as well as comedies such as *The Office*, have brought £123 million to the corporation's coffers. The collective sales income of the BBC was US$4.82 billion in 2002 (Transnationale.org). The commercial success of the BBC shows that it reaches many households across the world, helping to expand the representation of a certain aspect of 'Britishness'. It also shows that public service broadcasters can produce not only quality but also popular material.

Under the current regime, the BBC is allowed to use its revenue by investing it in more content provision and other businesses. In other words, profits are re-invested into this publicly owned organization. However, if this form of revenue became the only one available, then the independence the BBC enjoys today would be seriously jeopardized. Further, it would not be in a position to introduce experimental work, new directors or even programmes that are aesthetically unique or distinct, or that deal with controversial or 'difficult' material. The EU has made a clear commitment to the protection of public service broadcasting but it is at the discretion of member states to take the appropriate measures (the responsibility, therefore, lies with them). Britain has been governed by neo-libertarian politics for the last 20 years, and it has been one of the few countries in the EU to oppose protectionist measures for the cultural industries. If the past offers the best indicator of future performance, then there is very little reason to expect any policies in favour of public ownership in the media landscape.

The public service broadcasting system, and the BBC in particular, are facing a continuing threat, where the system is destined to be deemed 'obsolete' under the neo-liberal, market-driven ethos of British politics. It appears that the same forces that restricted the development of the broadcaster to a responsive medium of true public ownership are now accusing it of being unpopular or inflexible. Being under the control of government – to different extents over time and in various forms – the BBC has not been able to become a medium that is engaged with its publics. To do this, it would have to develop a greater degree of responsiveness to the needs of diverse audiences, and treat them as citizens rather than customers or market niches. It should be brave enough to encourage innovative programming and be ready to take risks. Under such circumstances, the BBC would embrace films such as *Injustice* and would be able to work alongside independent and grassroots content makers.

Bibliography

Ahmed, K. and Barnett, A. (2002) The Deal that Put a Porn Baron in Favour with No 10, *Observer*, 12 May.

Albert, M. (2002) Alternative Media: What Makes Alternative Media Alternative? in *Zmag* http://www.zmag.org/whatmakesalti.htm, accessed 3 June.

Allen, D., Rush, R. R. and Kaufman, S. J. (eds) (1996) *Women Transforming Communications: Global Intersections*, Thousand Oaks, CA: Sage.

Alternative press in Britain, subscription links (includes *Do or Die* and *Red Pepper*), at http://www.ink.uk.com/.

Anderson, B. (1983) *Imagined Communities: Reflections on the Origin and Spread of Nationalism*, London: Verso Editions.

Article 19 *Lagging not Leading: Freedom of Expression in the United Kingdom* in http://www.article19.org.

Atton, C. (1999) A Reassessment of the Alternative Press. *Media, Culture and Society* 21: 51–6.

Atton, C. (2003) Organisation and Production in Alternative Media. In S. Cottle (ed.), *Media Organisation and Production*, London: Sage.

Attwood, F. (forthcoming in 2004) Pornography and the Internet: Re-reading Pornography. In K. Sarikakis and D. K. Thussu (eds), *Ideologies of the Internet*, Cresskill, NJ: Hampton Press.

Banisar, D. (2001) *Freedom of Information and Access to Government Records Around the World*, Privacy International March 2001, at http://www.privacyinternational.org.

Barendt, E. and Hitchens, L. (2000) *Media Law: Cases and Materials*, London: Longman.

BBC, *Producers' Guidelines* http://www.bbc.co.uk/info/editorial/prodgl/.

Blumler, J. G. (1998) Wrestling with Public Interest in Organized Communications. In K. Brants, J. Hermes and L. van Zoonen (eds), *The Media in Question*, London: Sage.

Briggs, A. (1995) *History of Broadcasting in the United Kingdom*, Oxford: Oxford University Press.

Briggs, A. and Burke, P. (2002) *A Social History of the Media: From Gutenberg to the Internet*. Cambridge: Polity.

British Board of Film Classification, *Policy*, at www.bbfc.org.uk.

Broadcasting Committee (1923) *The Sykes Report*, London: HMSO.

Broadcasting Committee (1925) *The Crawford Report*, London: HMSO.

Broadcasting Committee (1962) *The Pilkington Report*, London: HMSO.

Broadcasting Standards Commission (1998) *Codes of Guidance*, at http://www.bbc.co.uk/info/editorial/prodgl/.

Bromley, M. (2001) The British Media Landscape: European Media Landscape. *European Institute for the Media*, at http://www.ejc.nl/jr/emland/uk.html#2.

Browne, D. R. (1999) *Electronic Media and Industrialized Nations: A Comparative Study*, Ames, Iowa: Iowa State University Press.

Burch, E. (2002) Media Literacy, Cultural Proximity and TV Aesthetics: Why Indian Soap Operas Work in Nepal and the Hindu Diaspora, *Media Culture and Society* 24: 571–9.

Byrne, C. (2003) PCC Investigates *Star* Donkey Story, *Guardian*, 5 November.

Campaign for Freedom of Information, at http://www.cfoi.org.uk/.

Chomsky, N. (1997) What Makes Mainstream Media Mainstream? In *Zmag* at http://www.Zmag.org.

Collins, R. (1994) *Broadcasting and the Audio-Visual Policy in the Single European Market*, London: John Libbey.

Collins, R. (1999) European Union Media and Communication Policies. In J. Stokes and A. Reading, *The Media in Britain*, London: Macmillan.

COMAG (2003) *Insight* (October) at http://www.comag.co.uk.

Commission (1994) *Background Report: The Information Society*, ISEC/B/17, Brussels.

Communications Law Centre (1997) *Access to the Media and Right of Reply*, Melbourne: Communications Law Centre Limited.

Copola, M. *Spare Rib* Magazine (1972–1993): Representing the 'New' Woman, at http://www.feminist-seventies.net/absparerib.html.

Council Directive (1989) *Television Without Frontiers*, 89/552/EEC. OJ L. 298, 17 October 1989.

Council of Europe (1950) Convention for the Protection of Human Rights and Fundamental Freedoms, as amended by Protocol No. 11, 1998.

Croteau, D. and Hoynes, W. (2000) *Media Society, Industries, Images and Audiences* (2nd edn), Thousand Oaks, CA: Pine Forge Press.

Curran, J. (ed.) (2000) *Media Organisations in Society*, London: Arnold.

Curran, J. and Seaton, J. (1997) *Power Without Responsibility: The Press and Broadcasting in Britain* (5th edn), London: Routledge.

Curran, J. and Seaton, J. (2003) *Power Without Responsibility: The Press and Broadcasting in Britain* (6th edn), London: Routledge.

Danziger, C. (1986) The Right of Reply in the United States and Europe, *International Law and Politics* 19: 171.

Datamonitor (2001) *2001: iTV Revenue Streams and Business Models*, London.

de Gouge, O. (1979) Declaration of the Rights of Woman and Female Citizen. In D. G. Levy, H. Applewhite and M. Johnson (eds), *Women in Revolutionary Paris 1785–1795*, Urbana: University of Illinois Press; also in *Modern History Sourcebook*, at http://www.fordham.edu (accessed 27 February 2002).

de Moragas Spa, M. and Garitaonandia, C. (1992) *Decentralization in the Global Era:*

Television in the Regions, Nationalities and Small Countries of the European Union, London: John Libbey.

Department of Trade and Industry and Department for Media Culture and Sport, at http://www.communicationswhitepaper.gov.uk/.

Dicken, P. (2003) *Global Shift: Reshaping the Global Economic Map in the 21st Century*, London: Sage.

Downing, J. (1984) *Radical Media: The Political Experience of Alternative Communication*, Boston, MA: South End Press.

Downing, J. (2001) *Radical Media: Rebellious Communication and Social Movements*, Thousand Oaks, CA.: Sage.

Doyle, G. (2002) *Media Ownership*, London: Sage.

Duncombe, S. (1997) *Notes from the Underground: Zines and the Politics of Alternative Culture*, New York: Verso.

Dworkin, A. (1981) *Pornography: Men Possessing Women*, London: The Women's Press.

Dworkin, A. (1996) Against the Male Flood: Censorship, Pornography and Equality. In D. Allen, R. R. Rush and S. J. Kaufman, *Women Transforming Communications: Global Intersections*, Thousand Oaks, CA: Sage.

Eldridge, J., Kitzinger, J. and Williams, K. (1997) *The Mass Media and Power in Modern Britain*, Oxford: Oxford University Press.

Enzensberger, H. M. [1962] (1995) *Einzelheiten I, Bewusstseins-Industrie*, Frankfurt am Main: Suhrkamp Verlag (English translation: Enzensberger, H. M., *The Consciousness Industry*, New York: Seabury Press).

EPI (Economic Policy Institute) (1999) *The State of Working America 1998–99*, Ithaca, NY: Cornell University Press.

EPI (Economic Policy Institute) (2000) *The Data Zone, Recent Economic Data*, at http://www.epinet.org.

Euromedia Research Group (1997) *The Media in Western Europe*, London: Sage.

European Communities (1997) Directive 97/36/EC of the European Parliament and of the Council of 30 June 1997 amending Council Directive 89/552/EEC on the coordination of certain provisions laid down by law, regulation or administrative action in Member States concerning the pursuit of television broadcasting activities, OJ L. 202, 30.07.97/ 60–71, at http://europa.eu.int/en/comm/dg10/avpolicy/twf/9736_en.html (accessed 25 May 1998).

European Court of Human Rights (1992) *Case of Castells v. Spain*, REF00000357, 23/04/1992.

European Court of Human Rights (1996) *Case of Goodwin v. United Kingdom*, REF00000559, 27/03/1996.

European Federation of Journalists (2003) *Eastern Empires: Foreign Ownership in Central and Eastern European Media*, Brussels: European Initiative for Democracy and Human Rights and European Federation of Journalists.

European Parliament (1982) Resolution on Radio and Television Broadcasting in the European Community. In *European Communities, Official Journal of the European Communities* OJ No C87: 109–12, 5 April.

European Report, Nos 2343, 2350.

Feintck, M. [1999] (2001) *Media Regulation, Public Interest and the Law*, Edinburgh: Edinburgh University Press.

Fero, K. (2002) Interview with Katharine Sarikakis.

Focus (2002) *World Film Market Trends*, Strasbourg: European Audiovisual Observatory.

Fountain, N. (1988) *Underground: The London Alternative Press 1966–1974*, London: Comedia-Routledge.

Franklin, B. and Murphy, D. (eds) (1998) *Making the Local News: Local Journalism in Context*, London: Routledge.

Freedman, D. (2001) What Use is a Public Inquiry? Labour and the 1977 Annan Committee on the Future of Broadcasting, *Media, Culture and Society* 23: 195–211.

Frost, C. (2000) *Media Ethics and Self-Regulation*, London: Longman.

Fukuyama, F. (1992) *The End of History and the Last Man*, London: Hamish Hamilton.

Galtung, J. (1999) State, Capital and the Civil Society: A Problem of Communication. In R. C. Vincent, K. Nordenstreng and M. Traber, *Towards Equity in Global Communication: MacBride Update*, New Jersey: Hampton Press.

Galtung, J. and Vincent, R. C. (1992) *Global Glasnost: Toward a New World Information and Communication Order?* Cresskill, NJ: Hampton Press.

Garnham, N. (2000) *Emancipation, the Media and Modernity*, Oxford: Oxford University Press.

Gitlin, T. [1983] (1994) *Inside Prime Time*, New York: Pantheon

Glasgow University Media Group (1982) *Really Bad News*, Glasgow: University of Glasgow.

Global Financial Data (2000) Historical economic data, at http://www.globalfindata.org.

Goodwin, P. (1998) *Television under the Tories: Broadcasting Policy 1979–1997*, London: British Film Institute.

Goodwin, P. (1999) The Role of the State. In J. Stokes and A. Reading (eds), *The Media in Britain: Current Debates and Developments*, London: Macmillan.

Guardian Media Guide (2003) ed. S. Peak and P. Fisher, London: Atlantic Books.

Guardian Unlimited, at http://politics.guardian.co.uk.

Hamelink, C. J. (1994) *The Politics of World Communication*, London: Sage.

Hamelink, C. J. (1995) *World Communication: Disempowerment and Self-Empowerment*, London: Zed Books.

Harcup, T. (1998) There is No Alternative: The Demise of the Alternative Local Newspaper. In B. Franklin and D. Murphy (eds), *Making the Local News: Local Journalism in Context*, London: Routledge.

Held, V. (1970) *The Public Interest and Individual Interests*. New York: Basic Books.

Hesmondhalgh, D. (2000) Alternative Media, Alternative Texts? Rethinking Democratisation in the Cultural Industries. In J. Curran (ed.), *Media Organisations in Society*, London: Arnold.

Hill, J. (1999) Cinema. In J. Stokes and A. Reading (eds), *The Media in Britain: Current Debates and Developments*, London: Macmillan.

Hosken, F. P. (1996) Women and International Communication: The Story of WIN News. In D. Allen, R. R. Rush and S. J. Kaufman (eds), *Women Transforming Communications: Global Intersections*, Thousand Oaks, CA: Sage.

http://www.geocities.com/SoHo/Cafe/7423/altpress.html.

http://www.indypress.org/links/.

Human Rights Watch Women's Rights Project (1995) *The Human Rights Watch Global Report on Women's Human Rights*, New York.

Humphreys, P. J. (1996) *Mass Media and Media Policy in Western Europe*, Manchester: Manchester University Press.

Husband, C. (ed.) (1994) *A Richer Vision: The Development of Ethnic Minority Media in Western Democracies*, Paris and London: UNESCO and John Libbey.

Hutchison, D. (1999a) Remoulding Public Service Broadcasting: The British Experience, *Canadian Journal of Communications* 24(1).

Hutchison, D. (1999b) *Media Policy*, London: Arnold.

Index on Censorship for Free Expression (2002) *Britain: Libel Laws Used to Curb Web Protests*, at http://www.indexonline.org/indexindex/20021219_britain.shtml and *Independent*, 18 December.

Index on Censorship for Free Expression (2003) *Rebel Hearts Heed Authority's Words*, at http://www.indexonline.org/news/20030203_a2z_survey.shtml, 3 February.

Itzin, C. (ed.) (1992) *Pornography, Women, Violence and Civil Liberties: A Radical New View*, Oxford: Oxford University Press.

Jaques, R. (2001) ISPs get an Eyeful of Porn Bonanza, at http://www.vnunet.com (10 September).

Jenkins, H. (2002) Interactive Audiences? In D. Harries (ed.), *The New Media Handbook*, London: British Film Institute.

Johnson, B. (2003) Don't Rely on Embedded Journalists, Urges BBC Mine Victim, *Guardian*, at http://media.guardian.co.uk/broadcast/story/0,7493,959356,00.html (20 May, accessed 1 October 2003).

Kleinwaechter, W. (1999) The Cyberright to Communicate: A Human Right of the Fourth Generation? In R. C. Vincent, K. Nordenstreng and M. Traber, *Towards Equity in Global Communication: MacBride Update*, New Jersey: Hampton Press.

Library of Congress, Accredited Women Correspondents in the Second World War, at http://lcweb.loc.gov/exhibits/wcf/wcf0005.html, accessed 25 February 2002.

Liebes, T. and Katz, E. (1993) *The Export of Meaning*, Cambridge: Polity Press.

Lippman, W. (1930) *Public Opinion*, New York: Macmillan.

Macdonald, M. (2003) *Exploring Media Discourses*, London: Hodder Arnold.

MacKenzie, J. M. (1984) *Propaganda and the Empire: The Manipulation of British Public Opinion 1880–1960*, Manchester: Manchester University Press.

MacKinnon, C. (1985) Pornography, Civil Rights, and Speech, *Harvard Civil Rights–Civil Liberties Law Review* 20(1): 1–70.

Madgwick, P. J. (1990) *Introduction to British Politics* (3rd edn), Cheltenham: Stanley Thornes.

Martineau Society, at http://www.hmc.ox.ac.uk/societies/MartineauSoc/martineausoc.htm.

Masmoudi, M. (1979) The New World Information Order, *Journal of Communication* 29(2): 172–85.

McQuail, D. (2000) *McQuail's Mass Communication Theory*, London: Sage.

Media History Project, at http://mediahistory.emn.edu.

Middlemas, K. (1996) *Orchestrating Europe*, London: Fontana Press.

Millar, S. (2002) Privacy Rights Swept Aside, *Guardian*, 11 June.

Morley, D. (1980) *The Nationwide Audience*, London: British Film Institute.

Nelson, E. (1989) *The British Counter-Culture 1966–1973: A Study of the Underground Press*, London: Macmillan.

Nordenstreng, K. (1999) The Context: Great Media Debate. In R. C. Vincent, K. Nordenstreng and M. Traber, *Towards Equity in Global Communication: MacBride Update*, New Jersey: Hampton Press.

NUA (2002) Office of National Statistics: Nearly Half of all UK Households now Online, at http://www.nua.ie, 17 December.

NUA (2003a) Datamonitor: Broadband Adoption on the up in Europe, at http://www.nua.ie, 20 May.

NUA (2003b) Nielsen NetRatings: Global Net Population Increases, at http://www.nua.ie, 25 February.

Office of Communications, at http://www.ofcom.org.uk/.

Ó Siochrú, S. (1999) Democratic Media: the Case of Getting Organized. In R. C. Vincent, K. Nordenstreng and M. Traber, *Towards Equity in Global Communication: MacBride Update*, New Jersey: Hampton Press.

Petley, J. (1999) The Regulation of Media Content. In J. Stokes and A. Reading (eds), *The Media in Britain: Current Debates and Developments*, London: Macmillan.

Philo, G. and Miller, D. (eds) (2001) *Market Killing*, London: Longman.

PMN (2003) Porn to be Major Driver of 3G Adoption, at http://www.pmn.co.uk/20030121adult.shtml, accessed 24 July.

Press, A. (1991) *Women Watching Television*, Philadelphia: University of Pennsylvania Press.

PressWise, at http://www.presswise.org.uk.

Raboy, M. (1995) Public Service Broadcasting in the Context of Globalisation. In M. Raboy (ed.), *Public Broadcasting for the 21st Century*, Luton: University of Luton Press.

Radway, J. (1984) *Reading the Romance*, Chapel Hill, NC: University of North Carolina Press.

Read, D. (1992) *The Power of News: The History of Reuters 1849–1989*, Oxford: Oxford University Press.

Reith, J. (1924) *Broadcast over Britain*, London: Hodder.

Rense.com (2003) Non-Embedded Journalists Say Beaten, Starved by US, at http://www.rense.com/general36/ssob.htm, accessed on 2 November.

Rogers, M. (1998) Moguls Past and Present. In N. J. Woodhull and R. W. Snyder (eds), *Media Mergers*, New Brunswick: Transaction Publishers.

Ross, K. (1996) *Black and White Media: Black Images in Popular Film and Television*, Cambridge: Polity Press.

Ross, K. (1997) But Where is Me in it? Disability, Broadcasting and the Audience, *Media, Culture and Society* 19: 669–77.

Ross, K. (2001) All Ears: Radio, Reception and Discourses of Disability, *Media, Culture and Society* 23: 417–9.

Rush, R. R. (1999) Theories and Research to Live by: Communications and Information in the 21st Century. In R. C. Vincent, K. Nordenstreng and M. Traber, *Towards Equity in Global Communication: MacBride Update*, New Jersey: Hampton Press.

Sarikakis, K. (2000), Citizenship and Media Policy in the Semi-periphery: The Greek Case, *Cyprus Review* 12(2): 117–33.

Schlesinger, P. (1991) *Media, State and Nation: Political Violence and Collective Identities*, London: Sage.

Seymour-Ure, C. (1996) *The British Press and Broadcasting since 1945* (2nd edn), Oxford: Blackwell.

Shaw, C. (1999) *Deciding What We Watch*, Oxford: Oxford University Press.

Smith, A. (ed.) (1974) *British Broadcasting*, Newton Abbott: David & Charles.

Spiller, P. T. and Vogelsang, I. (1996) The United Kingdom: A Pacesetter in Regulatory Incentives. In B. Levy and P. T. Spiller (eds), *Regulations, Institutions, and Commitment: Comparative Studies of Telecommunications*, New York: Cambridge University Press.

Sreberny-Mohammadi, A. and Mohammadi, A. (1994) *Small Media Big Revolution: Communications, Culture and the Iranian Revolution*, Minneapolis: University of Minnesota Press.

Statewatch (2001) Press release: *Special Report on EU Plans to Amend the Schengen Information System*, at www.statewatch.org/news/2001/nov/19sis.htm, accessed 7 February 2002.

Stevenson, N. (2000) *The Transformation of the Media: Globalisation, Morality and Ethics*, London: Longman.

Stokes, J. (1999) Publishing. In J. Stokes and A. Reading (eds) *The Media in Britain: Current Debates and Developments*, London: Macmillan Press.

Stokes, J. and Reading, A. (eds) (1999) *The Media in Britain: Current Debates and Developments*, London: Macmillan.

Sutcliffe, B. (2001) *100 Ways of Seeing an Unequal World*, London: Zed Books.

Think Tank (1994) *Report by the Think Tank on the Audiovisual Policy in the European Union*, Luxembourg: Office for Official Publications of the European Communities.

Thompson, K. (1997) *Media and Cultural Regulation* London: Sage (Open University).

Thrall, T. A. (2000) *War in the Media Age*, Cresskill, NJ: Hampton Press.

Thussu, D. K. (2000) *International Communication, Continuity and Change*, London: Arnold.

Traber, M. (1985) *Alternative Journalism, Alternative Media* (Communication Resource No. 7, October), London: World Association for Christian Communication.

Transnationale.org, at www.transnationale.org.

Tunstall, J. and Machin, D. (1999) *The Anglo-American Media Connection*, New York: Oxford University Press.

Turow, J. (1992) *Media Systems in Society: Understanding Industries, Strategies and Power*, New York: Longman.

Van Dijk, J. (1999) *The Network Society*, London: Sage.

Vincent, R. C., Nordenstreng, K. and Traber, M. (1998) *Towards Equity in Global Communication: MacBride Update*, New Jersey: Hampton Press.

Virtual Alternative Media Project, at http://www.uky.edu/Libraries/vamp.html.

Von Glinski, S. (2002) *25 Jahre 'Emma'. Alice Schwarzer rennt für die Frauenbewegung* (25 Years of *Emma*. Alice Schwarzer runs for the Women's Movement). In *Südwestdeutsches*

Rundfunk, at http://www.swr.de/thema/archiv/020126_emma/index.html, accessed 11 July 2002.

Wagner, L. (1989) *Women War Correspondents in World War II*. Westport, CT: Greenwood Publishing Group.

Wahl-Jorgensen, K. (2002) The Construction of the Public in Letters to the Editor: Deliberative Democracy and the Idiom of Insanity, *Journalism* 3: 183–204.

Watt, N. and Maguire, K. (2003) Mandelson Advised on Campbell's Departure and the Demise of Spin, *Guardian*, 1 September.

Wearden, G. (2002) Rural Areas Face 20-year Wait for Broadband, at http://news.zdnet.co.uk/story/0,,t269-s2103764,00.html.

Werden, F. (1996) The Founding of WINGS (Women's International News Gathering Service): A Story of Feminist Radio Survival. In D. Allen, R. R. Rush and S. J. Kaufman (eds), *Women Transforming Communications: Global Intersections*, Thousand Oaks, CA: Sage.

Westlake, M. (1994) *A Modern Guide to the European Parliament*, London: Pinter.

Weymouth, A. (1996) The Media in Britain. In A. Weymouth and B. Lamizet (eds), *Markets and Myths: Forces for Change in the European Media*, London and New York: Longindman.

White, A. (2002) Media Monopolies Versus Editorial Independence: Signs of Hope in Korea. In *OpenDemocracy*, at http://www.opendemocracy.net, 30 January.

White, M. (2003) MPs Urge Retreat on Unpopular Policies, *Guardian*, 2 September.

Woodhull, N. J. and Snyder, R. W. (eds) (1998) *Media Mergers*, New Brunswick: Transaction Publishers.

World History, at http://www.fsmitha.com.

Zmag, http://www.Zmag.org (extensive database of alternative media).

Index